TOTAL QUALITY
MARKETING

For Julie. The only person I know who delivers quality in such quantity. Thanks again, darling.

TOTAL QUALITY MARKETING

What Has to Come Next in Sales, Marketing and Advertising

JOHN FRASER-ROBINSON

with
PIP MOSSCROP

KOGAN PAGE

First published in 1991

Kogan Page Limited
120 Pentonville Road
London N1 9JN

British Library Cataloguing in Publication Data

A CIP record for this book is available from the British Library.

ISBN 0 7494 0389 6

Typeset by J&L Composition Ltd, Filey, North Yorkshire
Printed and bound in Great Britain by
Biddles Ltd, Guildford and Kings Lynn

Contents

Part One: A Question of Quality

Part Two: Heading Back Beyond the Year 2000

Part Three: In Preparation

Part Four: Methods to Make Changes

Part Five: On the Road to Quality

List of Figures

List of Tables

Acknowledgements

Pip Mosscrop: Pip, many thanks for your help and guidance in Part Four. Most especially, thanks for caring enough to join in and see if we could make a dent in the problem. Indeed, thanks to Collinson Grant for sharing its market-leader knowledge and skills, and not forgetting Hugh Dayton for the input on remuneration.

Andrew Macmillan: Andy, you were a great researcher. You came to me when I had little time to give, and you demanded none! A godsend. Your work was clear, wise, well-constructed and a dream to work from. Thank you. May you have all the success your skills deserve.

Christina Unwin: If you aren't the fastest, most accurate typist in the world, you ought to be! Thanks, Chris. And thanks for the weekends too!

To Andy's friends at the libraries of Bognor Regis College, Chichester, Brighton and Portsmouth Polytechnics; and, of course at IBM's Communications Library at North Harbour (especially to Valerie Sangwine); to IBM, Rank Xerox, Olivetti, Royal Insurance and all who have shared their stories with me (or Andy); to Clive and Edwina at Dunn Humby Associates; to Professors Phil Kotler and Lou Stern at Northwestern University, Evanston, Ill.; to Ursula and Walter (who didn't know it, but got me started on this track); to all those valued Clients who have given me the opportunity to assist with their problems (and learn some more about the meaning of life); to all those kind people who let me use, abuse or mess with their material ... yes, to each and every one of you ...

Thank you.

The object of a business is not to make money.
The object of a business is to serve its Customers.
The result is to make money.

Part One: A Question of Quality

1

The False Premise of Excellence and Quality

Do you work in a *quality* business? Or a *quantity* business? Is it possible to work for a business that is both?

Since Peters and Waterman wrote *In Search of Excellence* in 1982, the business world is alleged to have been heading towards a quality age. The fact is, there is, as yet, little evidence to show that quality standards overall are really improving. It seems more as if we were managing to regain lost ground rather than actually to improve quality. This has made me somewhat suspicious of the claims for the power of total quality management.

You see, I come from the jaundiced school that says 'If man does not have a great enough perception of what quality is, then no amount of training can teach those who are deficient in appreciation of such standards to deliver them.' Moreover, if you examine the excellence and quality movements in detail you will see that what they really offer is to turn back the clock, applying the standards of bygone days to today's profit-based, materialist age.

The premise is that if you get back to product supremacy through quality, you cannot fail. Sadly, it is a false premise. For, it would only work well if we were indeed living in a quality business age, but we are not. We are living – today – in a transitional age: the crossover time between quality and quantity. Not that these qualities are absolutely mutually exclusive. But, I fear, they are a lot more so than the likes of the excellence or the total quality brigades would have us believe.

You may think these views extreme. Then take off your business hat and ask yourself, as a consumer, how many genuine quality businesses you know. If you can think of one, or perhaps even two or three, where you are constantly impressed, not just with what they do but *how* they do it, you are doing well. And my guess is that you will be thinking of a business that puts its relationship building substantially in front of its business building.

These are the kind of businesses that share one of my philosophies about Customers. Namely, that it's far better to concentrate on what you do *for* Customers than what you do *to* Customers.

Such businesses are often one-man bands, relics of the age of craftsmen. They do a job for you at home, and they're a pleasure to deal with, leave no mess, make a skilled and exemplary job of the task, charge a fair price ... and it nearly always takes you months to get hold of them because they truly find it difficult to meet the demand. Of course! There is only one person there. Yet, if they should want to grow – and oddly few of them do! – how could they do it? Indeed, could they at all?

At the other end of the scale, multinational corporations, those who first abandoned these quality ethics for quantity, scale and size (and set us fair and square along 30 to 40 years of exploitation selling to deliver almost entirely to quantity-based objectives) are now seeking to go into reverse thrust. Except of course, being run by quantity-minded materialists, men and women who have climbed the corporate tree during the last 20 years or so, they find it difficult to shake off the old ways. Which is where the gurus of excellence and the dragomans of total quality come in.

As a result of all this, many people are now examining how a total quality ethic should affect their business. They are looking to see whether and how their business will improve from ideas such as total quality management.

Yes, we are dashing headlong into the age of quality: but what a pity! Because if ever a directional change needed thought and time, this is the one.

Many people will say – 'Wake up to reality. Our business doesn't have time to stand still and think.' Who mentioned standing still? Let's think on our feet. Let's, by all means, act 'quality' now – but let's also recognise what this means. For those involved in selling – and I cast the net as wide as it can be flung – this is a mammoth task. Selling has been quantity driven since time began; moreover, in the last 40 years, it has been quantity obsessed. This obsession has, in my view, led to practices and standards which can barely be justified. There is no mitigation. We are all to blame.

Over the next few years, the jury will give its verdict and the judge pronounce sentence. Our Customers are our judge and jury, and, following a period of relative peace and affluence in much of the civilised world, they have come to realise that they have the money. Therefore they call the tune.

Now that we have a 'global village' created by the media, there are no little comfortable corners in which to hide. What a shopper in Brisbane gets today, North Americans and Europeans see tomorrow and want the day after. The emerging world just wants to get to the front right away, but can't afford it.

For Customers who have the money or who have access to the credit, the world is theirs. Now the Customer can really be king. Not like that limp attempt a few made at it the last time. This time it's for real.

How can you change the way you sell?

Given the choice – and they will be – no Customer in his right mind would want to deal with a salesperson driven by quantity objectives. Customers already know that quantity objectives work against quality objectives. It is only those who sell to them who fail to do anything positive about this dichotomy.

Look at the classic high-commission businesses and the reputation they have: double glazing, timeshares, and perhaps even office equipment. There are many more such businesses, including, sadly, some of the financial services.

Acceptance of this basic premise – quantity objectives generally work against quality objectives – enables one to grasp the enormity of the change that must take place in selling, let alone in the whole spectrum of marketing for the quality-driven age – the age of excellence.

Consider it. For 40 years the once noble art of selling has tarnished itself by responding to the mindless call for more orders. It has become obsessed with 'pile it high, sell it cheap'. You may remember those words as the immortal utterings of Jack Cohen, founder of the UK supermarket chain, Tesco, a company now proud to boast that it is the greenest, cleanest, most Customer-attentive supermarket chain in the UK. Now Tesco sells quality. Or at least it thinks it does.

The future will cause many deep shocks. The pressure put upon business people by quantity objectives has caused many heart attacks. The pressure put upon businesses by quality objectives will cause a new phenomenon, the 'corporate coronary'. It happens as a result of a business's trying hard to keep up with the global levels of Customer demand; often it will quite literally fall to the ground dead: out of funds, out of time, out of energy; exhausted and exasperated. You will see the evidence unwind as this book progresses. You will equally learn how to avoid such a corporate heart attack yourself – or perhaps how to avoid being that trapped and tragic victim, an employee of a stricken company.

Everyone is talking about change; indeed, everyone is writing about change. I am going to be no exception. For the quite remarkable fact is that few have yet started to explain or describe the changes that will take place in selling, advertising and marketing. No one, to my knowledge, has produced any serious evidence or advice as to how those changes which have already been predicted will affect the people involved. Yet, I maintain, that now even the companies must themselves change to deliver quality in all aspects of marketing – advertising, selling, promotions, public relations and all the other facets of their communications and processes of persuasion.

When you see the need to change, then you have to ask this question – how can you change the way you sell?

Is it back to the drawing board?

Yes and no. For many salespeople, myself included, in the way that we operate, it is indeed back to the drawing board. But like so many other facts of business life, it is first of all a question of back to the board.

Quality, as has already been demonstrated by the other founding fathers of the movement, is a board matter. Perhaps, now that it has reached the marketing zone, it has actually become a matter even for the shareholders. For, it often requires mountains of courage and a massive financial investment.

We shall look at these points in more detail again. My point is that it cannot be some short campaign. It's no good putting quality on the topics for training for a month or two. This is not merely a question of how well you survive the next 40 years; it is *whether* you will survive to see the next 40.

It has taken 40 years for the pendulum to swing in the quantity direction. In my view, it is quite likely that the quality direction swing could last almost as long. I will show you my evidence. It is fascinating and convincing, and it points the way to your future.

So who has to change? And how?

The kind of changes we are talking about – what has to come next in selling, advertising and marketing – will be looked at in this book from many standpoints.

Take the salesman. (Incidentally, I use the term *salesman* and other similar words throughout this book in a non-sexist, gender-less sense, as a generic term.) How should he or she, the salesman, actually sell in the future? How will management change the environment, conditions and terms that sales employees work under to engender, measure and reward quality? How will the company restructure its sales and marketing teams to deliver quality, if restructure it must?

We will even take a fairly frank look at where quality wants to be sold. And where it wants to be bought. We'll look at why quality is considered a luxury at the moment, and how quality changes the Customer's basic needs and desires. We'll consider where, perhaps, a partnership approach might be more appropriate.

We will examine the view that selling is not about a single sale. Nor even is it about a series of sales. It is about success through satisfaction; the achievement of sales success through delivery of satisfaction to the Customer.

It is therefore a matter of perspective. When the seller and the buyer have different perspectives, their starting points in negotiation are on opposite sides of the fence. When they are both on the same side, trust grows, loyalty abounds, and success is a natural result.

New methods for you, new directions for your business

We are about to embark along an exciting and provocative journey together. If you sit back and observe and do the thinking, I'll drive and show you around. I'm perfectly sure you'll find great comfort in all you read, although a great deal of the contents may challenge you, your thinking and your practices. In which case I will have had my say and you will have had value. For this is the true purpose of this book: to change things for the better for you.

How much you agree with, how much you accept, how much you think about, how much you change is ultimately your decision.

Lastly, though it might seem obvious, I'll say it none the less. Don't look for the switch. There isn't one. There is nothing anybody can or will flick to change the environment from quantity to quality. It is truly a pendulum; possibly even a 40-year pendulum. Some people will do some of the things you are going to read about. Some will not. Some will do all. Some none. Some will do them tomorrow. Some in five years' time. The only thing you need to know about this pendulum is that it is relentless, in fact, unstoppable.

A revolution is about to begin. Sales, advertising and marketing people cannot escape this revolution. The Customer is in control. He can take his business anywhere. The survivors, the winners, will be those who master the new techniques and learn the ways of total quality marketing, and, therefore, what has to come next in selling, advertising and marketing.

Part Two: Heading Back Beyond the Year 2000

2

The Starting Block

The business of prediction gets harder as the rapidity of change increases. Thus, when you are dealing with a medium like TV, which gives you instant live access to your audience, you have the benefit of talking in 'real time'. A book, of course, affords neither reader nor writer such a luxury. For both of us, therefore, the task is harder. And, of necessity, we must limit ourselves to the major trends.

Certainly, by the time you are reading this, some of the things I predict will have started to happen; some of the stories I tell will have long since happened; and some of the events I report will no longer be happenings of such great significance. No matter. They will serve to show you the route and path of the trend. You can use your more up-to-date knowledge, or the ability to avail yourself of such, to enhance or modify the situation that exists as I write.

Indeed, as I write, what is the situation in marketing, selling, advertising and their allied areas? And what model shall we take to position ourselves for the off? Where, for instance, do I position myself against the classic arguments that still mystify or mislead some, particularly US and European companies.

Classic and traditional

Despite what follows in this book, I have to own up right away and position myself with the more classic and traditional marketers. Hence I will quite happily align myself with the school of thought that says marketing should control sales; sales is indeed a function of marketing. Having had the benefit of so extensively researching the future, and being able to set that in the context of the past, I feel strongly that even if you are sceptical of such a view now, you will come to agree with it very shortly.

You will not be alone whichever camp you are in. There exist many companies who see marketing and selling as separate, if associated, tasks. In such companies you often observe that a sales/marketing equivalent of the sales/production 'battle' exists. Sometimes as boyish playfulness (whatever sexes are involved!) and sometimes as outright war. Occasionally, a sort of strained professional co-existence prevails, and very, very occasionally a complete, mutually accepting, respectful partnership.

Equally, as another example, there are some people who regard advertising as above or below 'the line'.

Above, below or across?

The above views are neither classic nor traditional. They are as antiquated as those wonderful old socio-economic groupings that Britons should have abandoned years ago – A, B, C1, C2, D and E. Happily, as the creators and protagonists of this invisible line have ridden into the peaceful sunset of their sheltered retirement housing, we no longer need to grapple with the intriguing notion that sales promotion or direct marketing is 'below-the-line', or for that matter, that TV and the press are above it.

My position, as you may have guessed, is that I believe there should never have been a line. Certainly, again I use this word advisedly; there will be no line, or evidence that there ever was one, in the future. This may be just as well, for I suspect that many of the inventors of new media, such as the California-based SoftAd Corporation, would have greatly resented a below-the-line position.

SoftAd is typical of the enterprising new media we shall see opening up in the next decade. The SoftAd product, when I first came across it, was one of a kind. It is certain to spawn look-alikes, because it's such a great concept. The idea is to give or mail a computer disk to prospects instead of the conventional letters, brochures and flyers. SoftAd has developed special interactive software so that the recipient can play with or interrogate the featured products or services. The result is something of a TV commercial, brochure, mailing and direct sales call all in one. People often spend 20 or 30 minutes with your ad – so you can imagine the recall, the depth of product knowledge, and the potential relationship that could be established through such an idea.

To some extent, of course, the growth of this kind of product must depend on the growth of the personal computer market. And SoftAd certainly hopes so, since the figures it's working on show worldwide PC growth of:

1989 – 40 million
1992 – 125 million (estimate)

SoftAd believes that the companies who distribute high-quality information to buyers to help them make an intelligent, informed decision will be the ones who will prosper in the future. Direct marketers who have been able to use database techniques to make their messages more appropriate and relevant to their readers must agree with this.

The people at SoftAd, if I am any judge, may all be rich and famous by the end of the 1990s. They seem to have one of those 'right product, right time' opportunities which should yield them a long and healthy future. Yet, as we shall see later, you can be sure of very little these days.

Forget the future; where are we now?

Let's just put the future on one side for a moment and consider where exactly we are now. What stage have communications reached – whether for advertising, selling, Customer recruitment, retention or repair?

Having spent some time specialising in the direct marketing field, I have found a convenient 'yardstick' there. Because direct marketing relies so much on other aspects – computers, machinery, printing processes, all the creative tasks of photography, typesetting, and so forth, it's probably quite an interesting and valid example to consider.

Back in the 1950s, soap coupons worth just a few pence each were distributed the length and breadth of the UK by direct mail. These days, no one would even think about it. They would use house-to-house distribution for that task. And probably they would harness one of the increasingly sophisticated targeting systems to select the audience which most carefully matches the known profiles of their Customers. Using addressed, stamped, direct mail would no longer be considered viable, effective, or worthwhile simply to disseminate low-value soap coupons.

In the 1950s, advertisers would happily send out a mailing of 250,000 identical packages, distinguished only by the names on the outside of the little brown envelopes which carried them to market. Such users still exist, but they are few. And not many are left in brown envelopes!

By the 1960s, that same organiser of the 250,000 mailing was looking at new capabilities. Increased knowledge about the market, increased mechanisation of mailing lists, increased recognition of the importance of market sectors, and – I think – increased postage, had combined to make greater cost-effectiveness both necessary and possible. One way to achieve such was to break down the market into groups, and for the sake of the rest of this example, let us quite hypothetically imagine they are all the same size. So our friend would now mail perhaps 250 different mailings of 1000 within the total of 250,000. As that decade passed by, so the next held equally new opportunities.

By the 1970s, we were drawing well into the age of computerisation. People across the world were being exhorted to put their lists onto the computer. I remember how we used to balance out the number of times the list would be used, against its size, and the likelihood and number of selections that might be required to help a Client decide between staying on a manual system, choosing the mechanical addressing systems, or the infant but capable computer complete with all its teething problems. (Oddly enough, the manual system remains the only method still outside the UK and, I believe, some other European Data Protection Acts.)

Problems or not, the benefits far outweighed them, and so we had moved into the next phase. Now our friend's 250,000 mailing could consist of 1000 different mailings of just 250 like packages. This was the beginning of the age of personalisation, an age which was finally to be unseated and replaced only towards the end of the 1980s.

During the 1980s we saw the blossoming of the laser printer. In those few years it changed from the rather unreliable $500,000 10-metre box, to a desktop at less than $5000. Moreover, as the direct marketing industry grew, aligning itself alongside the computer industry, so the software market grew more sophisticated; together they provided extremely capable, multidisciplined marketing databases for everyone from the large companies with millions of Customers to the one-man band with only a few hundred or even fewer.

The growth in direct mail also warranted research and development in other production technologies; thus, there is now mailing-enclosing machinery which will take a whole range of different leaflets, brochures, and other enclosures and, based on the letter being sent, enclose the relevant materials with each letter. New technology equipment is thus used in conjunction with high-capability software, mailing programmes and accurate data-bases. You can understand why I explain to audiences that we have transcended the age of personalisation and arrived at the age of individualisation; for there is no reason why each person in the mailing should not receive an offer, proposition, message or whatever, which is entirely individual to him, cognisant of his circumstances, and recognises all the multiple facets of his individual relationship with the advertiser. So now we truly do see how that mailing, in fact, comprises 250,000 completely individual mailings.

But this is not the only evidence of the age of individualisation. For this is also the time when, while the motor trade in Germany asks three months to take the order for your precise specification of car and then deliver it to you, in Japan, you can have your own individualised car in just ten days. In two years it will be down to five days.

In the US, one refrigerator manufacturer, I'm told, asks you these questions before supplying you with your equipment. After all, who else would want it!

1. How big is the gap you wish to fill?

2. Describe your family's eating and drinking habits. Particularly, tell us about:
   a) cooled drinks;
   b) salads and fresh foods;
   c) frozen foods.

3. Please send examples of your kitchen décor. Any exterior colour can be matched; toning shelf and interior materials will be offered before building.

4. Please tell us which of the following you would like built into your unit:
   a) stereo radio/cassette/CD player;
   b) black-and-white or colour TV;
   c) video.

At the last question you might decide they've gone too far. After all, designing a unit that reflects the family's consumption and actual storage needs is one thing; trying to turn the fridge into an entertainment centre is something else. Not so, says the company. Its research shows that almost 70 per cent of equipment ends up with a radio, TV or tape player on the top. All the company does is organise your kitchen for you as an individual or individual family.

As time passes, you will see the phenomenon of individualisation grow larger. It's inspired not just by the producer's ability to harness design and manufacturing technology, and to deliver such products, but also by the consumers' need to differentiate themselves and their belongings in an increasingly uniform and dehumanised world.

So that is where we are: the age of individualisation. And that is, in many ways, the starting point for our time together. Glance around you now. Find where you and your business are. Remember it well, because the future holds some difficult and frightening times in store, times of uncertainty and high risk. You will remember these times for the ease with which you could do business, the ease with which you could make money ... and the ease with which you could satisfy your Customers. Times will change beyond all recognition.

Far be it from me to put the fear of God into you about the future, but that's exactly what I think might need to happen. I have pointed, as indeed have many others before me, to *change* being the cause of this fear. Not just change itself, but the rate, frequency and scope of change.

A definition of change might be 'making or becoming different', but this is not quite what I mean. I would like to place far greater emphasis on the future inconsistency and unreliability of the status quo. It will be the status quo for a decreasing amount of time. This means, in turn, that things you used to rely on – product life cycles; a competitive edge; Customer loyalty; material sources, prices, and suppliers; and so on – all these will become unreliable and untrustworthy in the next decade.

In such circumstances you must look to make youself stronger, more resilient. I have two suggestions for this. The first lies in your marketing process, the second in the quality of what you use your marketing to create. Specifically, I am referring to the quality objectives of your marketing. For, an aspect of the quantity/quality discussion we have not considered is this. Quantity builds sales. Quality builds friends.

Marketing is a three-way process

For marketing to achieve its full, effective power and to provide you with its full benefit, I believe it must be a three-way process (see Fig. 2.1). Your marketing should stretch forward to your

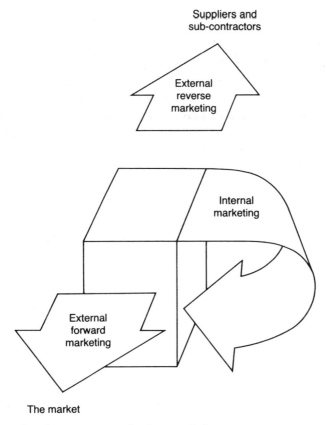

Figure 2.1: The three-way marketing model

market, inside to your employees, and behind you to your suppliers and subcontractors.

Let's examine this notion a little further.

Although I believe the need for marketing towards our Customers and prospects – the marketplace – is well accepted, I'm not sure the other two directions are. These are marketing to our own colleagues (internal marketing) and to our suppliers and subcontractors (reverse external marketing).

In relation to internal marketing, we are really considering the role, involvement and influence of marketing, training, and even some personnel and recruitment matters. These are areas which have a bearing on, or direct contact with, the market and therefore, in effect, become part of the product or service.

Reverse external marketing is born of, and generally reserved for, times of scarce or limited resources when it is used to ensure continuity of supply and, as far as possible, maintenance of price. I remember first seeing this technique used tactically during the three-day weeks and power rationing caused by the industrial disputes which hit the UK in the 1970s. A major heating and ventilating equipment manufacturer simply switched its whole marketing effort into reverse thrust and as a result surprised both its market and its competitors by making optimum use of its own limited production times. Not only was its resource planning careful, but somehow it always seemed to have the wherewithal to manufacture while the other firms were making more excuses than equipment.

In another time altogether, while carrying out a consultancy project for a supplier of office, factory and warehouse equipment, I discovered a company who, by tradition, seemed to care more for its suppliers than its Customers. At the same time, as if defying gravity, this company was one of the most successful, solid, and profitable I have ever encountered! It was also on a precipice. But that's another story.

The moral of both these examples is that supplier relations are crucial to delivery of the Customer promise and, as such, in my view, merit planned strategic marketing. You may feel that to run this kind of marketing continually, when I have referred to it as being excellent in times of resource shortage or threat, may be a little extreme. That depends on your resources and your suppliers. But the fact that I am suggesting *all* corporations should provide for this in their total marketing effort serves to underline the seriousness of my warning in relation to change and the extent and suddenness with which it will strike.

What factors will most affect marketing up to the year 2000 and beyond?

When we examine the factors which will most affect marketing up to the year 2000 and beyond, we discover some rather predictable old friends – such as the economy – and some new ones. Indeed, the whole thing is a bit of a jigsaw. And it may only be when all but the very last few pieces are in place that you will start to resolve your own uncertainties and make decisions about your future. I intend to spend some time looking at these factors, because without this background you will not understand all the reasons for the change in marketing, and the extent to which all its facets, not just selling and advertising, will change.

The major points of this chapter relating to the marketing environment and how it affects the marketer for the run up to the year 2000 are:

- We have arrived at the age of individualisation. This relates to products and services, not just the media used to sell them.

- Quantity builds sales. Quality builds friends for your business.

- To be at its most effective, marketing should become a three-way activity aimed at:

  1. the external market;

  2. the internal market;

  3. the external reverse market (suppliers).

The Economy – Predictions for the Future

You don't have to be an optimist to look at economic predictions for the future, but, as the saying almost goes, it certainly helps. In fact, there are some well-informed gloom and doom merchants who would try the strength of even the most optimistic optimist. I think it was Clem Sunter who said, 'The economy will go up. Or down. But not necessarily in that order.'

One can feel the economist's problem. The world is now a seething mass of microeconomies and macroeconomies. Electronic systems and information technology have accelerated reaction times to the point at which one hot word in the US can wipe billions off the UK or other stock exchanges while ordinary people sleep the night peacefully away.

In my view, you'd have to be a complete lunatic actually to want to make cast-iron predictions for the economy during what I believe will be one of the most (if not *the* most) economically turbulent decades in history.

Being economical with the future

Perhaps that is the only predictable fact about the global, continental and national economies of the future. They will become *more* turbulent and then more turbulent still. It is an irony that it should be so, but history shows that 'progress' in itself does not generally improve economic stability; just the reverse. Particular situations, government policies, crop successes, etc may provide stability on a national or regional level – but one negative situation which causes reverberation on a global or continental basis will nearly always overshadow or overpower them.

One conventional analysis of our global economic future suggests low growth or no growth; yet several international forecasters dismiss this. Some valuable new markets are opening up, they point out, suggesting that the increasing number of countries with market-orientated policies will provide vigorous growth. One economist at a US bank in Los Angeles nailed his flag firmly to the mast, saying, 'The 1990s could be the most prosperous decade of the century.' Unlike almost everyone else, this renegade contended that stability would be one of the strengths of the 1990s and that we would not see 'the sharp ups and downs of the earlier cycles'. Much as I envy someone who can make up his mind and come out with a positive statement for the future, I find this one to be somewhat reckless and lacking in regard for the evidence, although I would love to be proved wrong, preferably by an optimist.

The truth is that one cannot foretell the future. There are far too many factors which muddy up the pool. I suspect, for example, that the greenhouse effect may wreak havoc through even the most informed and reliable forecasts. Global warming may cause crop failures in some areas, and perhaps within 20 years Eastbourne Villages will take that historic corner of East Sussex and turn it into the red-wine-producing centre of Europe, the UK replacing Bordeaux, and threatening California and New Zealand into the bargain.

Yes, the fact is, when you examine scenarios for the future economy, the honest conclusion must be – 'Who can tell!' But it doesn't stop them from trying.

The Deutsche Bank, prior to the reunification of the two Germanies, was prophesying that the economies of nearly all the advanced industrial countries would be forced to accept a huge influx of immigrants from the developing world – the bank said: 'By the mid-1990s we're going to see the strongest surge in migration ever witnessed on this planet.' Oddly enough, whereas the bank bases its notion on entirely different factors, again it is the global warming changes which may award this prediction the accolade of being correct. Being right for the wrong reasons may be the best that our unpredictable future will allow us.

The shrinking world is growing

Does going international represent an answer to economic uncertainty? After all, if you choose your countries carefully, at worst and at least it spreads the risk. Again – right answer, wrong reason.

There can be little doubt that more and more companies will want to be international. For, as business development speeds up, staying on top of a market, or keeping in front of a business will require strong presences across worldwide markets.

The global economy

In his book *The Borderless World: Power and Strategy in the Interlinked Economy* (Collins), Kenichi Ohmae suggests that the developed world has become 'an isle, an interlinked economy'. He points out, absolutely correctly, that the costs of marketing and technology have turned most advanced and contemporary companies into high-fixed-cost businesses. This means they must seek out global markets to justify those costs. This proves, he asserts, that globalisation is, ironically, the direct result of internal corporate economics.

Yet the cost of internationalisation is great. Unless you're Japanese, of course. If you are, with capital costing you barely a quarter of what some Westerners must budget to finance their spreading wings, you will find the payback a lot easier. A bitter irony, since when we start to consider the quality story, we will discover that the nation that best understands and makes a commitment to long-term paybacks and investment in a market for the future is Japan.

So we have a paradox. Small-to-medium-size businesses, those who are not yet international, may need to develop internationally to gain, regain or maintain their commercial high ground. Yet, at the same time, large multinational corporations are unbundling because they have found that the hierarchy-laden 'big is beautiful' approach doesn't work; they have become overmanaged, overcostly, distant from and inflexible to the Customer and his needs.

How can failure signpost success?

Even if you're smart, you too can only fail at predicting a precise economic picture for the future. But how can we turn such failure into a successful consideration of the economy in relation to your marketing for the future? The answer is simple. We must predict for unpredictability. Plan not to have a plan. Construct ourselves to be reconstructed. Be flexible. Flexibility is my answer to the problem. And we'll look at how to implement that shortly.

Although this book is not really limited to Europe, from whichever viewpoint you stand, Europe has an impact on both the marketer and the economy. I'd like therefore to pull in at this stage some thoughts which are relevant. Both items relate specifically to Europe: the blossoming East and 'the brand' and Europe.

Eastern Europe – new markets for old

New markets have the benefit of hindsight. They may not be able to look back at their own experiences, but they can look back on ours. New markets also have new problems. Old or mature markets solved their own problems along the way. Thus, the new markets should not make the most of these mistakes again. Of course, this does not mean that they won't have problems. It means they should have different problems. One of these will be the effect of 'fast forwarding' developments which have taken 30, 40 or 50 years to take place. The same process happens successfully, but it is condensed within a time frame of five to ten years. It's risky, but irresistible.

Eastern Europe is a new, developing market, a market which requires patience from the most impatient animal after property developers – the marketing man. Although the Japanese culture is very distanced from those of Eastern Europe, I believe it is the Japanese who are best placed to cream off the most substantial tranches of the Eastern European market.

The Japanese, to repeat myself, understand the philosophy of the long-term payback. The biggest product that can be sold to Eastern Europe is not cans of food, motorcycles, cars, clothing or computers. It is know-how.

Selling know-how – in effect, training managers and providing knowledge – is also the method which leaves East European national dignities and pride intact and creates a consumer for the hardware which is required. Japan is familiar with this notion: familiar with it and relaxed, comfortable and confident about it. Add this to the fact that in Eastern Europe the Japanese are already, by and large, the best regarded and most favoured nation, and then non-Japanese will begin to see the task in front of them. It gets worse.

To have a new market with a fat wallet would be ideal, but Eastern Europe does not have a fat wallet. A few may be created in the process of development, but not yet. What's more, the Eastern Bloc's internal credit line is poor to non-existent. The citizens don't have funds, the corporations don't have funds and the countries don't have funds. With almost half the leading banks in the world being Japanese, and with Japan's low capital costs, again, unless we see some substantial change in Japan's position, it is ideally placed to score.

I am no particular supporter of the Japanese. Indeed, in my view they, more than any other nation, fuelled the quantity spiral of the 1960s, 1970s and 1980s. But I guess that's like asking, 'Who's to blame, the pusher or the junkie?'

These comments are made for the assistance of those looking at Eastern Europe as a potential market. Without any disrespect to its citizens, one has to realise that in market and marketing terms, it is primitive. Many conventional or traditional marketing activities will remain difficult, impossible, or unnecessary there for many years. It is a market that needs help and partnership first. I fear that just as we are beginning to see the end of exploitation-based quantity-driven marketing here, some nations or some corporations will prefer to take their old ideas to the new territory rather than change and adapt themselves.

I therefore wonder whether the impact of Eastern Europe as a new market for Western Europe may be significantly less than many expect, and following on from that, therefore, whether the effect on the European economy may prove substantially less too.

The Non-European

In *European Business Strategies* (Kogan Page), the management consultant Richard Lynch looks at the costs and resources of building a Eurobrand. He rightly acknowledges the vast profits that can accrue to those who can pull it off. However, to quote directly from the book, 'It can be seen that Euro-brands do not guarantee profits and require, as one might expect, substantial and costly brand-building activity.'

Will the Germans still get to the beach loungers first in the year 2000? Will the British still cook the worst food? Will we still crack Irish or Belgian jokes? Who can tell! I expect so.

Inside each of us living in the European Community there is both a European and a Non-European. I suspect it will remain so for quite some time. The point here is that you may be able to change more legislation and rationalise more regulations with each new parliament, but to change people takes whole new people. In other words, generations.

The marketer who wishes to succeed in Europe must understand his own brands as well as the markets he serves. In time we may well develop a 'Euroconsumer' but we are not there yet. However, creating a Eurobrand does not need a Euroconsumer. Nestlé markets about 20 different blends of coffee in 20 different countries, each meeting what Nestlé has determined to be the preferred taste of that marketplace, yet they all sell under the same label.

I believe talk of the converging consumer to be premature. It is an invention of the EuroAd Agency, who would like an easy life. It may happen – it is happening – but it will take time to have a major impact on anything other than very long-term planning.

Understand your brand

I have suggested that you must understand your brand. If you are Rolex or Coca-Cola, you have a brand which crosses national frontiers. If not, you may still need to market first to the Non-European inside us. What's more, if you are looking to your marketing colleagues to sit beside you and help you create a Euroconsumer, then you may be bitterly disappointed. For, many of those colleagues have sales strategies aimed at ever-narrowing market tastes and specialities. They have moved down the steps from mass marketing to segmented marketing and have just got to grips with niche marketing. The 1980s ended on the trend of database marketing; this gave the ability to target, the information to understand, and the tools to cultivate the individuality of Customers, as distinct from the desire or need to weld them together into bigger groups.

Moreover, as you travel around Europe, or if you see EuroAds (those created to be a common film with nationally overlaid captions and voice-overs), you will become aware that different nationalities approach advertising differently. Nobody uses more plays on words than the British; few use sex more than the French; the Germans have a very laid-back, matter-of-fact style, and so on.

So where are the Euroconsumers?

Where one can pull Europe back together by means of economics is in conjecture about whether we are dealing with a Euroeconomy or a gathering of several different economies. For a while yet, despite what happens with currencies, each country will be better or worse at managing itself, and deciding how much it wants to tax its citizens and what the tax should pay for. Each country will have its own problems and dilemmas, and for the foreseeable future so it will continue. Indeed, as the likes of McDonald's, Benetton, and

Coke rampage across Europe West and East, this may be one of the major differences they must recognise. Some differences, I suspect, will remain forever:

Only in France will Crocodile Dundee's famous expression ever ring true – 'It tastes like Pschitt, but you can live on it.' Only in Spain will a BUM biscuit be a good one. And why shouldn't the Austrians drink twice as much milk as the Belgians; the Germans own three times more dishwashers than the Dutch, who own twice as many video cameras as the Belgians? Across the border the French are busy consuming almost twice as much butter as the Italians. Meanwhile things are even more affluent outside the EC, where the Swiss have installed an amazing 1.3 telephones per person – twice as many as in the UK. No one has yet successfully explained to me why, dull, dismal and wet, as it always is when I visit, Belgium has a remarkable nine times more freezers than Spain, which, by contrast, roasts me alive whenever I'm there!

Has the UK got it wrong?

A survey produced by the headhunters Saxton Bampfylde International suggests that with just two years to go, few UK companies were addressing the key issues as far as the EC and 1992 were concerned. It is alarming that of those companies surveyed, 35 per cent did not think the European market important, and only 41 per cent, felt the matter worthy of priority. The report, correctly in my view, reaches the conclusion that the UK may have committed a grave strategic error by investing so heavily in the US through acquisitions rather than keeping the huge market on its doorstep more clearly in its sights. Certainly, this criticism could not, I think, be levelled at any other EC member. Is the UK out of step or are its partners/competitors?

Actually, Europe is a seething mass of anomalies trying not to get out. And long may it stay so. Yet I fear it won't, because we're just growing our Euroconsumers right now. They're our youngsters. They seem much more relaxed about sharing their cultural values and quite happy to purchase the same things. Despite this, there will nevertheless be a growing use of pan-European media – if only because it's easier to get a pan-European message across to the consumer. In the business markets, for example, few pan-European trade media yet exist, so, despite the wastage, specialist pan-European consumer media will be attractive for reaching the other category who are among the front runners to becoming Euro-consumers: the business market.

Another interesting use for pan-European media is emphasised by one enterprising ad agency who overlaid what they call 'golden circles' over Europe. Prosperity, it seems, does not conform to national boundaries, although, interestingly, the agency found that Europe's wealthiest consumers live mainly within a 250-mile radius of Cologne, Germany. My own years of direct marketing experience, however, would remind me of the value of targeting and targeting criteria. I must pose the question: do the affluent French buy the same as the affluent Germans? Do affluent British and Belgians buy the same brands, fly the same airlines or drink the same wines? I think not. I think maybe never!

Some time ago I was consulted by a leading European tour operator who had suffered a major problem with the marketing of canal boating holidays in France. He had printed some leaflets and, as a classic low-cost solution to the language problem, had remembered to keep all the copy to the black, enabling language changes to be made with a single simple plate change, leaving the other three of the four-colour set common. Having paid handsomely for an English copywriter to come up with terrific copy, he had various translations made and then sat back and waited for the business to come in. Except for the British, they stayed away in their thousands!

After some research we were able to establish why. The copy approached these boating holidays as if they were a luxury item for luxury-minded people; for in the UK, to the British, that is what they were. Yet to the French domestic market they were not really luxury at all, just a good middle-class, middle-of-the-road product. Its big appeal to the French was that it was an activity holiday. Once sold as such, sales lifted off nicely.

The same was true of his German market where, far from being a luxury holiday, it was actually an economy package for those who couldn't afford the grand financial splash of the Côte d'Azur in high season. Of course, the copy, to a bemused, besandalled, rucksacked Rhineman, was totally wrong. Once adjusted to point out the fantastic quality despite the low price, the package sold well in Germany too.

I think we will see several types of products. Some will flourish with a Eurobrand headlining its marketing; others will benefit from retained national branding. Equally, some countries will more readily accept Eurobrands (or brands perceived to be foreign). It seems quite plausible that children will suck Eurobranded, Eurotasting confectionery, yet equally plausible that, in an adult market, Nescafé will succeed with one brand and many tastes. Other products have one taste and many brands.

If you look at the US for an example you will, of course, see many different courses being followed. Yet strong brands like Coke and Marlboro may not tailor their products like Nescafé, but they certainly tailor their advertising. One quite often sees a kind of ethnic advertising, that is, a particular approach to the Hispanic market, another for the Chinese – or Italian – or even Irish-descendant communities. Europe too has sophisticated advertising and marketing professionals who are increasingly capable of tightly targeting the message as well as the medium.

Why should you be big? How can you be beautiful?

In many ways, the argument for size is dwindling if you are a national or European company. It is only if you are a global company with a product which is largely standard that you still achieve the colossal economies of scale. Many now prefer to be beautiful rather than big, because to be beautiful you often need to make yourself more attractive to a greater number of smaller groups. This leads you to the false conclusion that to meet the likely economic profile of the future, you need to be small-to-medium-sized, manageable, adept and fast in reacting to Customer needs. Yes, all of these things. But the pressures on the managers of small-to-medium-sized companies will increase cruelly. More money for research. More money for technology. More money for developing long-term Customer care programmes. More money for breaking into and funding new markets.

What all of this demonstrates is the need to do away with mass production of products and replace it with mass production of know-how. Thus, small-to-medium-sized companies wishing to compete will need to look for partners or become available for acquisition. We will see a quite rapid decline in the number of small, independent companies as we start to grapple with Europisation and globalisation.

So how will marketers and marketing cope with unpredictable economies?

The root cause of the unpredictability is uncertainty. To cope with uncertainty, one must stay alert, fast and responsive. But above all else one must understand that the key quality will be flexibility. This quality will repeat itself significantly throughout our thinking.

The resilience lent by flexibility will be crucial to successful marketing in the future. The marketing director has to learn to live by a new creed:

> *It is better to control a big budget*
> *than to control a big department*

Inevitably, this means the use of more consultants, specialists and outside contractors and the reduction of the marketing payroll.

Although we cannot predict the vagaries of the economy, I do believe we can predict, or rather look back through history, to see how marketing reacts to different economic climates, or different economic corporate situations.

When the going gets tough, the tough get fired – or do they?

What normally happens to marketing spend and marketing departments when times are good, bad or indifferent? In my experience, the indifferent is the worst of all, but it varies across the disciplines. For example, a lot of direct marketers and sales promotion people see increases in spend on their disciplines in lean times, when advertisers want either to maintain sale-related activity because it's at the 'sharp end' or, in the case of direct marketing, because it is so measurable in terms of its cost-effectiveness that you see exactly what works and how well. This is a great comfort when money is tight. However, with only those odd exceptions, the reaction to unfavourable economic change is fairly predictable. The better the times, the more is spent. The harder the times, the less is spent. It's only when a real storm hits that the actual marketing force is affected, and heads start to roll.

In order, the trimming seems to go as follows:

- 1st: PR activities, sponsorship, etc;
- 2nd: advertising and mass-media spend;
- 3rd: direct marketing, sales promotion, etc.

When at last the hatchet starts to hover, PR seems to smooth-talk itself out of the number-one slot and into a fairly safe, dark corner, leaving a usually quite flabby marketing department to be attacked and slimmed down first of all. The sales department tends to be threatened while the others get fired. When the sales force start getting fired, it's generally either a time to panic or a sign of bad sales management being flushed out and replaced.

However, I suppose, quite understandably, we marketers are, as a breed, very reluctant to fire ourselves! The point is that this rather cosy attitude will not help us to attend to the changes with which we will have to cope in the future and to react as swiftly and decisively as we must.

By using subcontractors, specialists and consultants to a greater degree, we are left with control but without the greater part of the workload. In the later section to do with the advertising agency of the future, you will see how this, in time, will work hand in glove with the Client of the future, for ad agencies must undergo some radical changes before they can satisfy the Client of the future. Moreover, they must develop – and Clients must encourage them to provide – far better, far wider-ranging, strategic marketing skills.

To summarise, then, the economy in which you will have to operate, whether you are affected locally, nationally, across your whole continent or even globally, is equally difficult to predict because of the number of 'wild cards' in play at the moment. However, critically, we have established the following points:

- Economies will become more volatile and turbulent.

- One method of spreading risk is internationalisation – but it's pricey as well as risky. Partnership could be a better answer.

- Planning must include less rigid parameters.

- Eastern Europe may prove less of an opportunity than forecast.

- Brand-strength will remain significant, although greater understanding of markets and their individual relationships with brands will become more important.

- Euroconsumers will come for some brands later than others; for some never at all.

- Marketing departments will need to implement flexibility as the principal strategic quality for the future, enabling them to react decisively, rapidly and effectively. In other words:

> ***It is better to control a big budget***
> ***than to control a big department.***

● Advertising agencies must provide wider-ranging, more intelligent strategic marketing counsel for their Clients.

4

The Technology Holocaust

Why do I call my technology review 'The Technology Holocaust'? I've a simple enough reason. My experience suggests that each new generation of technology actually puts the previous generation to death, for nobody seems to want old software or hardware when there's new available. This is not merely the impatience of the users. The market – competitors in some cases, Clients in others – can exert an enormous pressure on you to invest in the very latest technology. I have already referred to the impending squeeze on margins. Undoubtedly, the galloping desire to adopt new technology will cause more than its fair share of this.

As I took the Royal Mail's roadshow version of my Marketing 2000 conference around the UK, one managing director told the assembled few how his company was in the throes of installing its third complete computer system inside a two-year period. As he told the story, his fellow delegates groaned in sympathy with him. They identified immediately with his pain. The disruption, the frustration, the time failures, and the chaos that he must surely have endured.

'Bugger that!' he cried. 'Think of what it's cost and then tell me how I recover the costs.' He went on to reassure us that you only embark on such drastic, repetitive installation of new technology if you absolutely have to. And he absolutely had to. His market, his competitors' capabilities, and the demands of his Clients forced his hand.

So I do see it as a holocaust. And perhaps until we find a technocrat who can resist new products, innovation, and the latest capability, in favour of the old kit that has been in force for two or three years, I feel inclined to let the title rest.

Marketing and information technology: two crazy, mixed up kids!

Why has marketing (as distinct from direct marketing) taken so long to make friends with computers? It must have held us back immeasurably. Somehow or other, the world seems to be full of companies and organisations which have marketing people (especially at the top) who don't speak information technology (IT) language. And equally, it must be said, full of IT people who do not understand, nor want to understand, marketing.

A fascinating research exercise was carried out in the UK in 1989 by the Dunn Humby consultancy. It specialises in pulling together the IT and marketing disciplines and functions of a business, and has developed some interesting methods of helping marketing to understand and make sense of its numbers. However, its report highlighted two critical gaps: firstly, a gap between the personnel of technology and that of marketing; secondly, a gap between the acceptance that technology must assist marketing and the knowledge of how it should help and what it can do.

I am grateful to Clive Dunn and Edwina Humby for permission to quote so much of the summary of their valuable report, although I have 'rearranged' it a little.

IT and marketing management both recognise that computer technology will play an increasingly important role in the marketing department in the next five years.

The use of computers in marketing or database marketing is not just about direct marketing and communication with Customers. Quite the opposite. These applications are considered fairly low priority in the grand corporate scheme. Management feels that database marketing needs to encompass most of the business functions for which marketing is responsible, from product development to market research and selecting channels of distribution.

The survey revealed that the number-one priority of the company is 'improved Customer care and knowledge' and that marketing has an important role in helping to achieve this objective.

Sales management and product measurement are vital to company success, and technology has already made a significant contribution to these disciplines. Sales management normally falls outside the remit of the marketing department. Product-management technology, while invaluable, has, without doubt, held any number of companies hostage. In some cases it has become a barrier to Customer-driven systems. The product and Customer views of data represent important but conflicting decision-support systems.

The sales management function, which is not generally

within the marketing department's remit, saw the greatest support from technology. According to marketing managers, most of this support is provided internally by the IT function.

There are only two activities which are both marketing's responsibility in most cases and use technology to a reasonable extent. These are 'management and measurement of products' and 'market research'.

The survey showed that both marketing and IT management expect to see real gain from investments in marketing technology before 1995. Retailers, in particular, anticipate a fast payback period. Manufacturers appreciate that they have the greatest distance to travel in order to accomplish these objectives by 1995, and most fear the consequences if they fail to achieve them. Financial services managers are so convinced of the major benefits of database marketing that they believe a discrete budget should be allocated to help build them.

The picture of marketing and technology today is not rosy. Barely one company in three has a full-time IT team dedicated to marketing (see Figure 4.1). Managers trying to develop marketing systems do not always know at the outset what data is relevant and what is not.

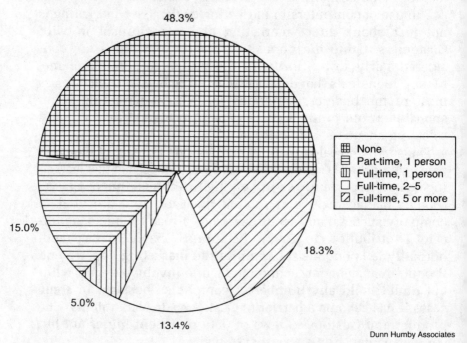

Dunn Humby Associates

Figure 4.1: The size of IT team dedicated to marketing

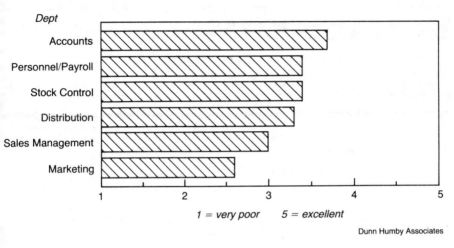

Figure 4.2: The view of IT management on communication skills by internal departments

Marketing managers feel that new skills are needed in the department. IT managers recognise the need for more training, particularly in helping them to understand the marketing process. No one doubts that today the marketing department is poorly served by relevant systems and expertise (see Figure 4.2).

The budgetary spend and limited number of marketing staff are features of a department highly dependent on third-party suppliers, particularly advertising agencies, market research companies and sales promotion agencies. And yet, clearly, no one is under the illusion that any of these third parties have any real knowledge or expertise in the field of marketing technology. Mainstream advertising agencies are seen as particularly naive – unaware of even the business benefits database marketing, or a marketing database, has to offer.

By contrast, direct marketing to Customers and prospects is much more technology orientated (62 and 51 per cent of companies respectively). More than half rely on a third party.

Clearly, marketing people need to communicate their technology requirements more effectively. It is not just about having a dedicated IT team.

Marketing is dependent upon information which is external to the business (market research, media costs, competitor intelligence, etc). Unlike most other data within the company, this marketing information does not tend to be transaction based; it's more likely to be statistical summaries (a collection

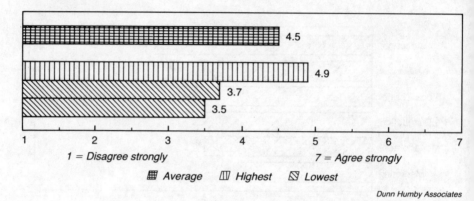

1 = Disagree strongly   7 = Agree strongly

▦ *Average*   ▥ *Highest*   ◩ *Lowest*

Dunn Humby Associates

Figure 4.3: IT staff have a poor grasp of the marketing process

of Customers sharing common characteristics). For this reason, and because the development of marketing systems is very new, the IT department finds it difficult to understand the needs of the marketing department (see Figure 4.3).

The survey quite clearly demonstrated that marketing managers expect the IT department to fulfil the role of adviser and provide the main focus of technology and systems development. The second choice of adviser are the specialist systems consultants. The bad news is that in many companies the development backlog on a major systems development is around one year.

Today the IT manager has a fairly poor opinion of the marketing department's use of technology. Even those departments rated 'above average' are still seen as the worst communicators among a number of other departments, including the sales department. The IT manager is aware of the potential problems which must be faced in 'getting to grips' with marketing. There are few concerns in terms of the available hardware or even software, although advanced software tools, such as CASE tools, do appear to help. The missing link is training and education and, in particular, knowledge of what makes marketing data different.

Some management is optimistic about the possibility of off-the-shelf software to help solve many of the difficulties, although this optimism is fairly half-hearted.

Quite clearly, there is evidence of database marketing in practice, mainly among the financial services and retailers. Nevertheless, it is early days for most practitioners. IT staff dedicated to the marketing department are few and far between. Where they do exist, they represent a first and major step towards developing new systems and analytical skills within the department.

There is little doubt in the minds of respondents that database marketing and the use of computers in the marketing department are set to increase dramatically. Indeed, many expect their company to have realised the full potential of such technology by 1995 – most notably retailers.

The two statements attracting the highest level of agreement overall were:

1. 'The marketing department must have user-friendly access to computer systems.'

2. 'Marketing will see an increase in the use of computer technology over the next five years.'

How, then, is this revolution to take place?

Over 48 per cent of companies surveyed do not provide a full-time IT team to look at the marketing department's needs. Also, the marketing management expects the internal data-processing department to be its main ally in the development of such systems. External suppliers came a very poor second.

Today, the marketing department's main use of technology is in relation to media selection and market research, and this is generally provided by third parties. The marketing department does not see any of its current suppliers as major partners in technology. The top three suppliers are advertising agencies, PR consultants and market research companies. Marketing managers gave a thumbs down to each of these as allies in technology.

Marketing managers actually rated the advertising agency's understanding of 'the potential business benefits of technology in marketing' as very poor. This must be a serious issue, since advertising agencies are in constant or frequent use by the marketing department. Certainly, they must at least understand 'the potential' of computers in marketing to stay as central as they now are to the marketing function.

Conversely, the IT manager is aware that he does not fully understand the marketing function; the answer evidently is education and training. All managers recognise that there is a long way still to go. They are mindful that they need to show results and payback as early as possible from corporate investment in technology and software systems.

The overwhelming conclusion of the research is the need for better communication between marketing and IT departments and relevant education and training. These two factors will undoubtedly lead to a new breed of business analyst, literate in both the marketing and IT disciplines.

The survey clearly proved that getting IT and marketing together is a task which is not made any easier by the fact that, while both sides clearly accept the need, they are reluctant to get started mainly because of the ignorance of each other's methods and work. Dunn Humby's excellent and pioneering work will no doubt help many to solve this and related problems. For, it is crystal clear that those who will be the successful businesses of the 1990s, those who will be leaps and bounds ahead as we cross to the new millennium, will be those organisations who can effectively marry their marketing and IT teams. In fact, it will be those who create a culture within their marketing departments for IT to thrive and grow in.

This must come from the top. I have not yet seen a successful company where the tone of the organisation's IT activities, and its whole attitude to IT generally, is not set at the very top. Although this doesn't mean that everybody from the top down needs to be at the leading edge of IT – it does mean that those without sufficient strategic and tactical knowledge of hardware and software will be likely to see the price of their ignorance in reduced profits later. This goes far deeper than merely understanding the media opportunities for which we can thank new technology. It is about understanding how – in all its widest aspects – technology can assist in the marketing function.

In tactical terms we are already seeing major advances, despite the fact that I have always found the consumer – with some notable specialist areas of exception – to be a lot less enamoured of technology. For a while, when the first automatic teller machines (ATMs) appeared, it looked as if nobody would use them. Not only is most cash now withdrawn through ATMs in the developed world, but new models are in production which enable you to transact your whole banking service that way. This is a possible alternative to the so-called 'Yuppie Bank', First Direct, which introduced 24-hour telephone banking to the UK.

With fewer than one in four companies having IT represented at board level, progress may slow a little, but never, in my view, to the speed preferred by the consumer. Undoubtedly, in Europe, the French lead the way; not only is their market alive to technology, but their consumers seem to delight in each new innovation. One wonders sometimes whether it has reached a level of technology for technology's sake.

At the beginning of the 1990s, the UK's NatWest Bank announced plans to spend over £1 billion on its computing and telecommunications in the first five years of the decade. Displaying his vested interest to the full, its IT director proclaimed the bank's computing centre to be 'the most important part of the bank's business'. While accepting his enthusiasm, everyone, whether in marketing or not, should remind himself that the most important part of any business does not actually lie within the business at all. The Customers of the business are, by far, the most important part. This is not some glib cliché. It is a fact – a fact which, despite decades of training and education, too many businesses still fail to recognise. Especially banks. These businesses are likely to receive their penalty within the next decade. Putting the Customer first is something that many people find extremely difficult. Cast your mind back. Have you ever been engaged in conversation with a so-called Customer representative when his phone rang? Who won – you or the phone? Usually, it's the phone. But why?

Micro or PC: which will win?

For the marketer, harnessing computer technology at this level – particularly with the versatility offered by local area network-linked PCs – would seem quite adequate. One reliable source estimated that the early years of the 1990s would show:

- 33 per cent compound growth in PCs;

- 61 per cent compound growth in those which were interconnected.

In the latter part of the 1990s it is anticipated that we will see the arrival of the supercomputer – a machine 100 times more powerful than those in common use at the beginning of the decade (and probably 100 times smaller!). Such machines will respond to voice, touch and probably gestures too. PCs will mostly be capable of full-motion video.

All of these features will serve to enhance the acceleration of the computer's acceptance at every business level. This is important, since one of the benefits we should look for from computers, especially in times of uncertainty and risk, is their assistance in speedily analysing market data as a strategic tool for creating insight, making discoveries and assisting forward planning.

In 1980 there were as few as 10,000 desktop systems. A decade later, in 1990, that had risen to 90 million and by the year 2000 you can expect that to double to 180 million. Unbelievable, but you'd better believe it! Most of these will incorporate DVI (digital video interactive) technology, full-motion video, mobility through cellular telephone technology, and three-dimensional quality graphics through imaging and rendering technologies. For example, this will enable:

- architects to show your new building on screen, with 3-D 'feel' to the images;

- scientists, engineers and designers to use similar visualisation to alter designs or ideas at will;

- travel, hotel and tour operators to show you full-motion videos and use computerised booking through the same screens and terminals.

Partnership ventures were mentioned in the last chapter as an aid to helping small-to-medium-sized companies cope with staying in front of their competitors. The whole concept of partnership as it affects both business-to-business and consumer marketing will arise again. As more and more organisations get together to work on collaborative ventures, we will see networks increase. IBM has predicted this will top 90 per cent of PCs, during the 1990s. Networks undoubtedly offer faster communications, wider access to information. Along with these benefits and crucial to collaborative ventures, they also support shared and decentralised decision making.

What happens to supercomputers – and how will they affect marketing?

During the mid-1990s, I fully anticipate the marketing world to become preoccupied with speed: speed of delivery, speed of response and reaction, and speed of innovation. This is because speed will for a while during the 1990s become an increasingly fashionable management technique. The so-called supercomputer will be used, to a large extent, to assist this, being used primarily to find product design and manufacturing solutions. Strapped to computer integrated manufacturing (CIM), we can expect super-computers to facilitate the product cycle and enhance individual-isation techniques. We will see robots employed in increasingly sophisticated applications requiring, perhaps, vision, navigation and manipulation; and all aspects of business will make wider use of artificial intelligence.

The pressure on marketers will increase from the manufacturing units enthused with their new capabilities. For in CIM plants, the computers will not only run the plant on a day-to-day basis, but they will also use their experimental analyses to develop new software and product design: all the while, they will manage and monitor the supplies resourcing, housekeeping, and all the logistics relating to materials and product shipment.

As you can imagine, it is quite possible that the largest inhibiting factor in all this will be education and training, for the technology is, in most cases, already beyond prototype.

A quick look at speed

I said that speed, as a management technique, would become a preoccupation for a while. It will also become a marketing preoccupation for a while. Let's consider the reasons.

There is currently a belief among some – predominantly US – management advisers that speed is a factor which can enhance or rather, in some way, turbocharge an organisation. In 1989, Kaiser Associates, which operates from Vienna, Virginia (US), surveyed 50 major US companies which had adopted speed strategies. Kaiser's belief was that speed was a competitor-killer. I don't doubt that Customers love it, although I hold a firm belief that a preoccupation with speed is fine from time to time but detrimental as a way of life. I have found that, used periodically, it blows away cobwebs and is a great shock treatment for corporate lethargy; however, when this preoccupation becomes a way of life, human nature obliges the cutting of corners and the failure of quality standards. It seems to me that speed eventually loses its per-ceived added value with a Customer as soon as each burst is added. Almost as if, in perception, the Customer sees each speed improvement as a step up, and is content to rest a while at the new level before feeling the need to move on again. Yet, even without the advantage of the supercomputer, technology is already providing speed increases at every level of business.

I think it was Domino's who offered a free pizza if it was delivered later than 30 minutes from your call. A terrific speed promise! They could hardly believe their eyes when in one isolated community an independent operator advertised, 'Why wait so long?' He guaranteed a 15-minute pizza. Apparently, Mr Enterprise had loaded an oven onto a van; the driver had a cellular phone, and as soon as you called he started driving and the man in the back started baking!

At the other end of the scale the facts are less amusing but more startling. Prior to the 1990s, General Electric had reduced to three days the order-fulfilment system that used to take three weeks to provide the box for an industrial circuit breaker. Motorola, according to a report in *Fortune*, used to take three weeks from order to manufacture its pagers; now it's down to just two hours. The design of a telephone at giant AT&T was once a two-year task; now it's halved to one year.

In 1989, IBM was deposed from its apparently unassailable position as *Fortune*'s 'Most Admired Company in its Industry'. The supplanter was none other than Hewlett-Packard, headed by one of the speed school's greatest advocates, the company's chief executive, John Young. Young was quoted as saying, 'Doing it fast forces you to do it right the first time.' At the same time, the Boston Consulting Group uncompromisingly asserted: 'If you come up against one of these fast corporations and you're not prepared, you're history.' Despite this Ramboesque rhetoric, the case histories in favour of the speed school build to an impressive list of graduates and masters. So it seems, as I feel obliged to point out, that not everyone shares my disenchantment with the 'way of life' prognosis for speed.

There are two sides to this coin. Let's appraise them. Is speed something you should align with periodically to maintain your rate of acceleration? Or is it a notion you should view as a permanent obsession? Ultimately, of course, it's going to depend what business you're in and what kind of business you want to run – not to mention the quality regime you wish to prevail.

If you're thinking of the speed technique ...

If you are thinking about the speed technique, here's some advice that may help you decide whether to investigate it further.

Think first – and think new

It's unlikely that you are going to make significant speed improvements by chipping away at existing processes, controls and systems. Radical improvements will come from radical thinking. Be sure to set yourself radical objectives. But, be warned, if you simply wind up the existing resources to go faster, they'll just burn out.

So think first. Take a long hard look at your business. Question long-held traditions; examine your sourcing; put every step under the microscope. Make a flow chart – look particularly at the administration and bureaucracy. Approvals are a particular and well-recognised source of delay and procrastination. Often they do more for the ego, than they do for the end-product.

Look at the whole operation

There's no point in cranking yourself up to a new speed and then letting your suppliers at the back end and your distribution at the other let you down. What's good for you is good for them.

Look for ways to worship speed

If you want your people to live speed, maybe there are things you can do to help them give it enough thought. Breed a speed culture. From the design of your offices, to the look of your lorries, to the out-of-work activities you encourage, or, maybe, even the sports that you sponsor.

Build in responsibility

The only way to ensure you don't lose quality as you turn the heat up is to make it abundantly clear to those responsible for it – and that's everyone. If you're in manufacturing, explore the 'right first time' and 'just in time' concepts.

Many people would recommend that a team-cultured business is best geared to cope with speed techniques with least risk to quality. All the evidence suggests that you can give teams difficult objectives; you can make teams responsible for the maintenance of their quality standards; but you must also give them the authority to make their own decisions. Being in control of one's own destiny is a true motivator.

Make a shrine of the schedule

Time is infectious. Taking a little more is tempting. Holding something over until tomorrow or just hanging on until the weekend's out of the way are habits with which 'speed' businesses cannot live. Speed requires commitment – nothing short of a serious act of God should put the schedule out! Lastly, remember what Carnegie used to say in the last century – 'The pioneers get scalped!'

The speed technique is, for me anyway, rather an overrated idea: one of those management fads which will come and mostly go. There will be those for whose business it may perform a miracle; but, in my view, the biggest miracles would be likely to be performed in highly predictable places. Would Motorola's managers be so delighted with their two-hour pager if they hadn't been happy before with a three-week pager? The answer could be that they were simply too bloated, flabby, bureaucratic and sleepy. Other forms of good management would have provided prevention, whereas speed provided a cure.

How open are the computer giants?

You may feel that technology is running fast enough. Yet it could run faster. For example, if we could get the computer giants to give in to the pressure for open systems, this would be one major advance – and I would imagine pretty much a global sigh of relief. In these days when so many industries have been able to introduce global standards, global reference systems, and global cataloguing, there is no real reason why the computer industry couldn't give us just one global computer language.

It was only vested interest and greed that stopped this innovation during the 1980s. Perhaps increased pressure from users will finally be successful. Currently nearest the mark is the AT&T-developed UNIX system. But there seems little point in switching from the IMB near monopoly during the years from the 1960s to the

1980s, to the AT&T near monopoly of the 1990s. My hope is that to
lock users in by unfair methods like this will not pay in the long
run. On the other hand, IBM sure has made it pay for the last 30
years.

Three major players in Europe

There was talk as long as ten years ago that there would by the year
2000 be only five major computer manufacturers in the world. In
Europe it certainly looks as though the homegrown talent will be
down to three. At the risk of losing a few friends, I predict there
will be for Germany – Siemens; for France – Bull; and for Italy –
Olivetti. None of them are without their problems. The early 1990s
has seen major restructuring by IBM (they spent £2.4 billion) and
Olivetti.

Changing shape for the future

There is massive evidence to demonstrate that restructuring of
companies for the future is both necessary and beneficial. We will
consider this in more detail separately since even if a company
does not totally restructure, marketing departments and sales
departments will have to, for the market already has.

Technology will both help and hinder this process. Ultimately,
the take-up of new technology will depend as much on the
consumer as anyone else. Very few consumers welcome new
technology simply because it is new. They seek only the benefits it
brings – a less direct demand upon the marketers of tomorrow, but
a demand none the less.

It was reported that in the 1988 congressional race in the US, the
California Democrat Anne Eshoo decided not to use TV and radio
ads like all her fellow Democrats and, for that matter, her
Republican competitors. Instead Ms Eshoo had her assistants and
party workers deliver 90,000 8-minute videos to undecided voters
in the Bay area. At just $1.22 each, they seemed good value. She
failed to win the seat, but scored 47 per cent of the vote, whereas
before the highest Democrat had only nudged 37 per cent.

Every time you turn round some new device is being launched
upon us. Laptop computers, interactive software that allows
computer owners to play with and interrogate advertising messages
sent on disk, supercomputers, global corporate teleports, robots

that feel – maybe soon the much heralded next-generation computer. If it is true that there are more scientists actually alive today than the sum total of those who have already retired to that great Silicon Valley in the sky, then I do not yet see the pace of invention and innovation slowing down to the pace of implementation.

In Chapter 4, regarding technology's influence on future marketing, we noted the following major points:

- Marketing and IT must work more closely together, and *both* sides must have a clear understanding of each other's objectives.

- Marketers will most likely favour LAN-linked PCs for day-to-day working. Major databases will be handled on higher machinery, but the flexibility and access of the PC is vital to successful marketing.

- Supercomputers will be adopted to speed up computer integrated manufacturing techniques. This, in turn, will put pressure on marketing departments to move more products and move them faster.

- Speed will become a fashionable management technique in Europe for the early- to mid-1990s – it will need thoughtful application to maintain quality.

- The introduction of 'open system technology' would be of significant benefit for marketers, who will mostly have to face restructuring of their department (if not their company), and this will put pressure on both the methods of communications and systems generally.

5

The Communications Traffic Jam

With all the new technology multiplying, with all the new media, we are inevitably heading for a potential communications traffic jam. So many people trying to say so many things, so many different ways, so many times, to increasingly *fewer*, in other words, more closely targeted, individuals.

The people I buy from want to communicate with me; the people I used to buy from are ringing and writing and knocking on my door. My fax machine responds to a caller who is trying to get me to be a Customer of his. The car phone interrupts the commercials on the radio which distract me from the posters telling me which paper I should buy to decide which TV channel I should watch. I think I'm getting mediaphobia!

But who cares anyway – I can zap the lot of them! Figures published in France show that technologically advanced homes (definition: those which have a remote-control channel changer) switch channels while the ads are on. Thirty-one per cent of these look around the other channels while 29 per cent just kill the sound. The birth of the silent TV ad is only around the corner. When you've got the ad, you simply show it on all channels simultaneously. Easy!

Seriously, I am quite convinced that this 'traffic jam' will become one of the most critical factors for marketers of the future. Why? Because it is the crossroads for so many of the other factors: communications, the media explosion, the 'technosplosion', the desire to improve Customer service, and so on and ever on.

To fan the flames of this burning issue, there is a common fallacy among marketers that more communication equals better service, and, equally, better service means more communication. It may be true in some cases, but the one is not a prerequisite of the other. I will, however, concede that very often more communication *feels* like better service.

Although I am no friend of the phrase 'junk mail', many people who are Customers of some of the more old-fashioned, direct-marketing or mail-order houses may still suffer from the seemingly endless bombardment of apparently untargeted mail that invades their homes. I doubt that any of these Customers would agree for a moment that more communications equal better service.

However, you can actually turn this issue the other way round and know you are on safe ground. Bad or low-quality communications will damage (or be perceived by the Customer to threaten) Customer service. The need therefore is to focus on, assess and prioritise the quality, method and validity of the communications. To overcommunicate or to miscommunicate generally will harm Customer relationships. Nothing gives a Customer a more telling idea of just how much a company cares for him than the organisation of its communications.

You may have experienced the appalling frustration of ringing someone with an enquiry or complaint and being passed around a building from extension to extension, each time having to relate your story yet again to someone who doesn't know you from any other of 2 million Customers. This is not a question of bad company organisation or structure. It is not necessarily a question of poorly trained or motivated staff. It is usually the sign of a company that doesn't appreciate that Customer service starts with having someone the Customer knows will be there. You know they know you. You know they will sort things out. You know they know what's going on in relation to you. *They* care about *you*.

Why is this so difficult – or apparently so?

Customers – consumer or business – need to be someone

Barclays Bank PLC in the UK tells its Customers that they have a personal banker. My personal banker doesn't know me. My personal banker is strangely absent when things go wrong. When things go wrong, the manager signs a form letter which was written either by a manager at the same branch in 1956 and has served well ever since, or possibly by the corporate form letter-writing officer: a gentleman (no woman could write such bilge) who plainly was away sick during the 1960s and 1970s when UK bank managers stepped out of cupboards in TV ads in order to disprove their traditional, old-fashioned and commercially inept image. Strange really, that as a school-leaver with some terrible financial ideas, habits, and desires, when I started to work, I enjoyed a relationship with my bank manager which verged on guerrilla warfare, but which was far more personal – and more satisfying. Why? Because hc kncw mc. He knew my problems. He knew what I was going to do to try to solve them. And, silly me, I got the distinct impression the hoary old buzzard actually cared. I'm not singling out Barclays in particular – although I may be singling out particularly the British. However, it does seem to me that this simple, basic financial need – a banking service – cries out to be made more human not less so; to require more recognition, knowledge and understanding; and to be made to be of optimum benefit to the Customer, whether delivered at a distance or not. None of this defies automation; rather, it requires it. It is the use to which the automation is put that must change. Why was it possible in the 1950s, but with all the technology and communications at our disposal in the 1990s, apparently neither available, achievable nor cost-effective?

Yes, why do more Customers mean less service?

It is another fallacy to believe that Customer service has to decline with the number of Customers being dealt with. Yet, in banking and many other services, automation and technology should have provided these suppliers with the means to maintain quality while profitably delivering service. It appears not to have done so.

So here is a classic Customer-service dilemma, one that many organisations would set about solving, just as Barclays has, by providing someone (or two!) who will speak to you personally, who can call up your information on their screen, who can pretend to know you. Your personal banker. And so they are. Just as soon as you tell them your number!

My Customer number should be number one, and so should all the others

Oddly enough, the Barclays example is only a fraction away from the right answer. It's just that banks should provide the service, not the lip service. I have dwelt on this example not because I have the answer but because marketers all need to consider how the problem is solved. To its credit, Barclays Bank has managed to avoid the obvious mistake, the campaign answer.

This is one of marketing's favourite solutions – to hit the problem head on with a campaign to prove to the Customer that no problem really exists. Thus, a campaign is mounted to make personalities of the various service managers at the bank, to hold 'open evenings' so you can meet all your 'friends' at the branch (they still need to give you a name badge!). And so on. Psychologists maintain that people often say the exact opposite of what they feel, want, or believe – this campaign is a classic example of the syndrome. Now you are encouraged to communicate with each individual 'expert' for each service. And, of course, they will do the same. You'll get letters from the insurance experts, phone calls from their investment experts – and the mandatory quarterly newsletter or magazine. You now have a standard Customer-service campaign formula at work on you.

How does it feel to be just another Customer, Mr Whatsyername?

You're about to enjoy the communications traffic jam. Junk mail from head office. More from the branch. Telephone calls when you least want them. And that's happening with almost every firm you use. Your bank. Your insurance company. Your travel agent or holiday company. All your credit card companies. And the department store, catalogue, and ... and ... and.

Hang on to your hats. In the next ten years, you'll see these messages come from your personal fax (or electronic mail system), your video phone ('tellyphone') – not to mention your PC link – and, of course, the interactive television. Super clean, hi-tech, fibre-optic lines will bring all this to your home complete with cable networks – all of which will offer you teleshopping and the latest in video mail order catalogues.

Who loves you, baby?

So who loves you? Is it the people who communicate the most, or the people who manage their communications best to build a satisfying relationship with you? The difference will be that the latter has a total communications management (TCM) policy, and therefore one person looks after you, understands your dealings and knows you. It happened in the 1950s, and now, thanks to our technology revolution and particularly the capabilities of sophisticated marketing databases and intelligent *internal* company communications, it can happen again.

TCM brings order out of chaos and someone who recognises you

The TCM strategy is as effective for the individual consumer, the family unit, or any scale of business. The fundamental realisation is that the communications are not there to sell in their own right (the cause of junk mail!); they are the means through which the interaction of the relationship will take place. There is absolutely no reason why they cannot be made to sell for you, but to do so effectively, you must recognise that selling, repeat selling or cross-selling to a Customer within the privileged, trusted position of a Customer-care or Customer-service programme is a very different activity with a very different tone and a very different style.

Did you notice that word *trusted*? What impact did it make on you? Does selling to an existing Customer feel like selling from a position of trust? This trust is perhaps most openly and obviously displayed, as I hinted earlier, in the way that you organise your communications with the Customer. Referring back to Barclays Bank, how can I trust, or give any semblance of credibility to a 'personal banker' who doesn't know me, doesn't know my name, doesn't know my financial position, nor even understand the background of my relationship with the bank? Plainly, I can't. The title exaggerates.

So, what do I mean when I suggest and repeat that the organisation of the communications is the shaft of realisation through which Customers will most quickly assess the true level of caring that goes on for them within any organisation? Simply this. The businesses which recognise you as an individual stand out from the crowd. They know that the most successful way to deal with you as an individual is to appoint an individual on their side to be the guardian of their relationship with you. Furthermore, and this is the truly distinctive aspect, in that single individual they invest finite control over all their communications with you.

Old-fashioned salespeople the world over will greet this comment with much glee and many 'I told you so's. Well, they should quieten down. They may have been right, but it is not possible that the businesses they worked for, employing them and rewarding them the way they did, could possibly have vested this power in them. For, to be truly effective, the controller of communications must also be the controller of the relationship generally. Few business practices of the last 30 years would permit this to happen because their structure, employee standards and the resulting regulations and safeguards would preclude it.

Just as manufacturing went into mass production to achieve greater efficiency and reduced costs, so, too, Customer service went into mass communications and mass-handling methods for the same reasons. All the trends are now in complete reverse, the methods of quality are to do with individualisation, not only in terms of the product or service, as discussed earlier, but also in terms of the relationship and recognition which is developed with the Customer.

TCM requires that all communications be ordered and enacted (or triggered) by the guardian of the relationship, since only this person knows, at any given moment, what the precise status quo is with any individual Customer. Thus, the Customer perceives that the right hand knows what the left is doing all the time. You are never passed on to an unknown or unnamed individual; you never leave the caring hands of your guardian. Never!

For those involved in mass mailings to Customers, however personalised those should be, this does not rule out anything that you are doing. It does make two important differences. Firstly, large bulk mailings to Customers must become a thing of the past. The wherewithal for those mailings are now placed at the disposal of the guardians. They, in turn, feed them in to the Customer communications programme at the optimum time. Secondly, the communications must be seen to emanate from the guardian, not from some central point.

Many who have discovered the quite exceptional cost-effectiveness of direct-marketing programmes to their existing Customers may worry that the cost will increase as bulk mailing postal savings and other savings disappear. However, they can be reassured that the benefits from improved timing and relevance generally far outweigh any increased costs. After all, no one can be in a better position to know when the timing is right than the guardian.

For those who have a logical product/service line extension, there is another valuable advantage. By logical product/service line extension, I mean a range of products for which a logical and progressive path of relationship building is possible. In many cases, such ideas are not even conceivable at the moment, but they become possible with the added closeness and intimacy of the relationships that result from TCM. Financial services are ideal for this approach; so are any kind of products where the taste and style of the Customer are an issue; or even those where apparently unlikely activities may seem foreign to relationship building such as in professional fund-raising. The ultimate product there is your last will and testament! Incidentally, my own experience in charity fund-raising, suggests that legacy income will increase beyond all bounds when the kind of techniques we have discussed here are in operation.

Let's take a run through the major topics of this chapter – as harmless as they might seem at the moment, they will prove to be among the most pivotal in your marketing of the future:

- We are in danger of witnessing (or becoming involved in) a communications traffic jam of global proportions. This will be caused by an increasing number of people wishing to communicate with the Customer and the rapidly increasing communications media and opportunities they will have at their disposal. This jam will alienate Customers and prospects alike.

- Customer-service levels should not decrease as the number of Customers increases. Indeed, the reverse should be true.

- Total communications management (TCM) provides an effective method of organising and controlling *all* communications with the Customer to maximum effect for the building, maintenance and growth of broad-based, successful and satisfying Customer relationships.

- TCM delivers improvements to marketing effectiveness by maximising all the elements of the Client relationship and thereby adding significant timing benefits to repeat-selling or cross-selling activities.

- Mass or bulk Customer communications (most especially mailings) will generally become a thing of the past. The materials or resources for them will be deployed to the guardians.

- Products or services which have a logical growth or progress path will show special benefits from TCM methodology.

6

The Media Explosion

Throughout the world we are seeing massive explosions in the growth of the media through which we marketing people can transmit our messages. This ranges from the growth of radio in Africa to the massive increases in television in Europe – not to mention the additional media which technology places before us.

Reproduced here (Table 6.1) is a chart, published in 1990, of the new television channels scheduled for launch in the UK alone. Almost 60 channels – and that's only broadcast television – not cable.

This number of channels is quite staggering when you think that each year, each channel might load onto the market up to 250,000 minutes of extra advertising airtime. This suggests that almost 60

Table 6.1: The timetable for new television channels as predicted in 1989 for the UK

Year	Method of transmission	Number of channels	Coverage
1989 (Feb)	Astra – medium powered satellite	16	National
1989 (Sept)	BSB – high powered satellite	3	National
1990	Eutelsat 11 – medium powered satellite	16	National
1991	Local television franchises by cable or microwave	Multiple (20)	Local
1993	4th and 5th Direct broadcast satellite	2	National
1993	Channel 5	1	70 % national
1993	Channel 6	1	Less than 65 % national

million airtime minutes of extra commercials might be beamed onto the unsuspecting UK citizen by about the mid 1990s. God forbid! There is plenty of conjecture about what will happen to prices; to jobs in the industry; to quality; to effectiveness. The media winners and losers of the future will depend on two pivotal issues. The balls are in the air at the moment. The future depends on where they land.

The future role of the mass media

In many ways the attributes of media will be measured differently in the future. Some of this has to do with the changing objectives of the marketers, as we will see in Chapter 15. A lot has to do with the fact that we have left the era of mass marketing, passed through the era of segmented marketing, and arrived breathless and slightly perplexed in the era of the niche market where we gaze at the arrival of individualised marketing with some apprehension.

It would be a strange irony indeed if, just as the television invasion climaxes, the advertising world were to decide it didn't need TV any more. I don't think that will happen. I suspect we are not discussing whether the media are used, but for what they are used and what proportion of spend they will command.

Many of the so-called below-the-line media have come to realise that they too can play a much greater role in both the brand- and corporate-building process. Thus, whereas once they concentrated solely on their tactical objectives, they now spread across both planes – tactics and strategy. This duality of role makes good economic sense. And it makes powerful advertising too.

The Marie Curie story

I learned this lesson from my late father. Thomas Bernard Robinson, OBE, founded the Marie Curie Memorial Foundation, more popularly recognised these days as Marie Curie Cancer Care. It's a somewhat romantic story, starting with the influence of Sir Winston Churchill, to whom my father directly reported towards the end of World War Two, and an old lady who, when hearing of my father's intention to start a cancer charity, took off her engagement ring and offered it to him. He sold it, as she had suggested, for about £75, in those days a reasonable sum for a first donation. However, my father decided to devote all of it to raising more money. So he carried out a mailing (although I suspect his early hand-picked, hand-signed missives didn't seem like direct mail to him!) to raise funds. It was successful. The amassed funds financed another mailing and so on until he had built a base of regular subscribers and enough surplus to start on the serious work of fighting cancer and caring for the stricken.

As the years passed, the professional marketing skills increased and Father learned, as all charities do, that the donor-base becomes the high-response, high-donation centre of activity, and the prospecting element the low-response, low-donation part. Indeed, it is quite often only the lifetime value of a donor that makes the prospecting effort worthwhile. I wonder why people expect marketing a charity to be any different from life! Many have found that one acquires a donor at a loss which is turned into profit later through reapproaches and perhaps trading in some way.

As the years passed, my father got more creative. He introduced a mail shot that covered ten houses at once (and effectively black-mailed each house into giving more than the last); a way to person-alise mailings before personalisation was economically viable, thus for many years turning the telephone directory into his top-pulling list; and – may we all forgive him – the charity Christmas Seal.

By now the Marie Curie was mailing its donor list (the word *database*, of course, was not invented for years to come!) twice a year, and 'cold' prospects mailings were dispatched by the millions – literally. At one point, I believe, he had the rate well in excess of 12 million a year; for one extensive period he mailed more than any other charity, and, certainly, for almost two decades more than any other cancer charity.

There were two side effects, both extremely valuable. Both, all these years later, hold a moral for all advertisers, especially those who use direct marketing.

Moral 1: He built up extraordinary loyalty from his regular donors, to the point where massive levels of legacy income were attributable to the long-term donors. In-deed, in the fund-raising world the correlation between loyalty-building, long-term donor mailings and legacy income is now well recognised.

Moral 2: The Marie Curie achieved the No. 1 slot in brand awareness. Its unprompted figures left the others light years behind! The learning point here is that he achieved this coveted position without spending any significant sums on advertising. The 'advertising effect' was achieved as a by-product of the massive mailings. It cost him nothing.

This example clearly demonstrates what many advertising traditionalists have been reluctant to admit. Direct mail, like many of the other marketing disciplines, can have a powerful effect on brand building, and an equally strong contribution to the process of loyalty building, which, as the marketing world refocuses on relationships, will be thrown under a greatly increased spotlight.

It can be seen that the media of targeted marketing can reach and address the niches, but can achieve their own objectives as well as some of those usually reserved for the mass media. I anticipate that the demand for hitherto mass-media objectives will increase through those media that have not been used to deliver them in the past.

So what of TV, the press and radio?

While there may be a decrease in some areas for the mass media, a small consolation might be drawn from the increasing prominence of the corporate position behind the brand. For, undoubtedly, as 'Western' consumers sophisticate and reappraise their buying criteria, we will see them look behind the brand to the corporation that owns it. The policies and practices of that corporation will be watched more closely, be discussed more intelligently, and be acted upon more aggressively. The Green movement is a perfect example – woe betide those who are tempted to pay mere lip service to Green values. When Du Pont makes it a declared aim to be a 'zero-pollution' company, the Greens, who, thankfully, suffer no fools gladly, will expect the pledge to be honoured.

I hold the sincere conviction that for the future such criteria will prove to be of major significance in corporate survival. The world's population is selfish enough to consider its own longevity to be of far greater importance than any corporation, or, for that matter, industry.

The mass media do seem to be de-massifying themselves to some extent. And, as I remarked earlier, the major conjecture lies around what will happen to them as they do. Europeans may look to the US for a model but should take note of the different position in relation to cable TV and also the fact that Europe is running behind. Therefore it is nearer the precipice of new technology.

In the UK, towards the end of the 1980s, the cost of production of television commercials rose at twice the rate of inflation, and the cost of TV advertising rose three times faster still. It is therefore reasonable to expect that prices will fall as some of those new channels get up and running. At first glance, certainly, if my career had been in selling for a TV company, I think I'd have looked to the mid-1990s for a good long holiday, probably paid for by the previous three decades.

However, if you look beyond that basic supply-and-demand conclusion, which suggests falling prices, the UK did follow the US model in the latter part of the 1980s, when available airtime effectively trebled with the advent of Channel 4 (the second nationally networked commercial channel), all-night television, and TV AM, the breakfast-time contractor. With this experience it became clear that advertisers were not so much interested in commercial minutes as in the right audience for their ads. With the further proliferation of commercial radio in the UK, following much the pattern of France and the US among the principal 'radio' nations, it is likely that the delivery of the right audience to the advertisers' expectation – either geographically or demographically – will assure the future of at least some of the new names on the airwaves.

Much the same view could be drawn of what is happening to the consumer press throughout Europe, although it could be argued that many European nations, particularly in terms of their magazines, have been prolific in these respects for some years. The UK reads less, but watches more.

Broadcast TV – the big threat

Reverting to TV, it is likely that the biggest threat to broadcast TV – ground or satellite – will come, not from other media, but from cable.

While the amount of TV increased in the UK the total audience for commercial TV did not. This simply meant that advertisers found it both more difficult and more expensive to achieve the coverage which only large audiences provide. And there are currently still plenty of advertisers needing such opportunities.

The biggest threat to broadcast TV undoubtedly comes from cable, certainly in the UK and, I suspect, over a decade span throughout most of Western and what is currently described as 'Eastern' Europe. I spent some time working on the strategic and creative elements of a US cable corporation laying down its tentacles in the UK. If you are creative, there is no greater delight than becoming 'sold' on the proposition yourself before having to sit down and get to work on the serious job of converting the rest of the world. A number of times in my life this has been quite hard. However, as a consumer, subject to the price and mix of programming, I am in no doubt that the superior option is cable, especially when you add, as the cable companies undoubtedly will, the telephone- and computer-link options – plus the inevitable home-shopping 'tele-logues'. TV has in the past enjoyed much of its success not as a result of its ability to deliver, but of agencies' inability to use their imagination. In the 1960s and 1970s their answer to almost any problem you handed them was either 'Let's do TV' or 'Let's do more TV'.

This was not the professional, unbiased, strategic counsel that Clients thought it to be. It was sheer unadulterated greed. The criteria were the agency's bottom line, (and the way they were remunerated, being a percentage of the media rates). During that same ten-year span, the rates climbed through the roof, yielding even greater profits. Who, among those agency ranks, would tell the Client to reduce or come off TV?

Ironically, despite this, TV advertising spend has moved from approximately two-thirds of total advertising spend to just one-third. TV was hoisted on its own petard. For, as the rates increased, Clients started to look for other, better-value options. Winking seductively at them were the salesforces and account teams of those so-called 'below-the-line' marketing service companies.

New media – where will the growth be?

Although we have spent most of this chapter looking at advertising media it would be far more realistic to look at communications media in general, since almost any medium can be put to an advertising or marketing use. Perhaps the one which instils least confidence for me was the enterprising farmer whose fields bounded the railway line north of Brighton in southeast England; he sold sides of beef, promising the target market of the travellers on the passing trains. I suspect the page-space value of the PR he generated as a result was greatly in excess of his eventual sales.

A good example of a medium that has been overlooked as an advertising medium is the telephone. Yet many claim this to be a selling rather than an advertising medium. This is not a semantic discussion. As the future unfolds, this is a discussion that you must join in. We will take some views later on.

New media will arrive in profusion as technology and communications capabilities grow. However, it is the use to which those media are put that will define their value to the advertiser, together, of course, with their success at capturing the hearts and minds of the particular segment or niche they call their own.

Decreasing value, decreasing cost-effectiveness

The most important point to note for the future is that almost all media – particularly the mass media – will follow the fragmenting market and endeavour to reach tighter targets. For this they will expect to chase a premium – in other words, rates per thousand (or whatever quantity) will undoubtedly increase. For marketers and advertisers among them, this means, by and large, that markets will become more tightly definable, but more expensively available: the classic advertising media generally will become less cost-effective, and I anticipate that they will attract less spending. The only possible area increasing its use of mass media against the general trend is the area of corporate image and positioning, an area which may at last come out of the airport corridor display case and into the mass media.

In this chapter we thought about the following factors and how they will affect us tomorrow and beyond.

● Media profusion is set to continue at explosion level for many years – particularly outside the conventional mass-media areas.

● Media will tend to follow the fragmenting markets to offer tighter geographic, demographic and sociographic definition. For a tighter economic price!

● Brand objectives can be successfully delivered by all media – as long as their strategic objectives are recognised along with the tactical. This is a realisation sadly much overlooked until the last few years – mostly by the marketing services community who controlled them.

● The 'brand behind the brand' – the corporation – will take on an increasing prominence as the consumer becomes more sophisticated and informed. Expect the Greens to take full advantage of this as they, and other consumer groups, gain in strength and influence at all levels of society.

- The 'right audience for your ad' will become more influential on the price an advertiser is prepared to pay. Quantity will be less influential.

- Cable TV, because of its aesthetic values (everything on the set and nothing on the roof) and its ability to offer computer and telephone services – all three at optimum-quality standards and without interference – could easily eventually become the predominant carrier, at least in urban and suburban areas throughout Europe.

- As more advertisers seek unbiased strategic marketing counsel, TV will find it difficult to retain favour and will probably lose out to those media who can deliver 'double-duty advertising', direct marketing and sales promotion, for example. Corporate advertising, at this stage, would appear to contradict this trend and increase its priority.

- It will generally get more expensive and need more organisation to reach audiences on a mass basis (although mass audience products will remain in quantity) – thus, many methods of advertising will become less cost-effective.

7

The Decline of Selling Ideas

This chapter covers ground that may be difficult for many to accept, not because its thesis is complex or hard to absorb, but because of the challenge it makes and the investment it requires.

Indeed, the next chapter – 'The Rise of Marketing Ideas' – will seem to exacerbate what certain people may choose to see as a prejudice against selling and sales ideas. It is, of course, difficult to point out weaknesses, suggest modifications or demonstrate new methods without some implicit criticism of the past or even the status quo. Thus, traditional salespeople could look at my career in marketing and claim that the grudge has tumbled out of my head and onto the page. I feel at least that if I make my personal position clear, then those who feel I have prejudice will at least have the measure of it.

I have always considered that I hold the strategic views of a marketer and the tactical skills of a salesperson. In relation to the art of selling, I have, when appropriate (and that was often), energetically and enthusiastically worked to bring a high level of professionalism to both of these. In my view, you can be a professional salesperson only when you have an understanding of both the value and process of marketing. Equally, marketers can fully appreciate the salesperson only when they understand that it is the salesperson, generally, who achieves the successful results which are the testimony to the marketer's ability. Despite this rather balanced disposition, it has never been difficult for me to accept that selling is a function of marketing.

I suppose that, from these views, you can clearly understand my long-standing interest in and involvement with direct marketing; it requires the two in absolute harmony. However, you may also appreciate my disenchantment in recent years when so many direct marketing practitioners have failed to understand the need for quality with quantity and have chased the Holy Grail of the cost per sale. You may also understand how the most recent years have led me to work for the re-establishment of quality as a primary marketing requirement!

What is selling all about?

Let's not beat about the bush. Let's leap in with both feet and alienate a whole group of people! Here goes ...

Selling is *not* about the Customer. Selling is about the product or service. This is actually neither new nor prejudiced thinking. In the late 1970s the eminent Professor Philip Kotler from Northwestern University, in his paper 'From Sales Obsession to Marketing Effectiveness', in the *Harvard Business Review*, suggested that 'Selling focuses on the needs of the seller. It is preoccupied with the seller's need to convert his product to cash.'

I own a factory. It makes widgets five days a week. By Friday the warehouse is full, and I have nowhere to put next week's widgets. I'd better get a salesforce.

'OK, salespeople, get out there and sell these widgets. The more you sell, the more you earn.' They clear the warehouse. But the factory goes on manufacturing, and the staff and the overheads need paying and the suppliers too. Better get the salesforce back because the warehouse is full again, and I need to collect the money they've raised from the first lot. In comes the salesforce. They leave the money and clear the warehouse again! This cycle goes on very nicely for a few weeks, except soon the salesforce seem to be having some trouble clearing the whole warehouse. 'We're selling as many widgets as we can, but it's getting harder to find new Customers, and we need something extra to tempt the existing Customers to buy more.'

'OK, Salesforce, give them a discount.' The warehouse is empty again, but only for a day or so; soon the relentless production at the factory has filled it up again. 'Get back here, salespeople – my warehouse is full again.'

'But it's only Thursday – and we've still got problems getting rid of last week's production.'

'Give 'em a BOGOF.'

'What's that?'

'Buy One, Get One Free! Now get out of here and get going. And don't forget to leave the money!'

As the salesforce clear the warehouse yet again, their eyes boggle. The warehouse is bursting at the seams, and the next week's production is filling up the shelves at one end as they're clearing the other. What can they do next to make the Customer buy more?

Selling has to manipulate to succeed

I have taken you through the Toytown example above to illustrate my point. Excuse its microcosmic simplicity, please. But you can see from this that Kotler is right. Selling is, or has certainly become, a manipulative and exploitative process. As I said in the introduction, it is obsessed with quantity. It sets its objectives by quantity. It rewards by quantity. It is an aggressive, offensive action.

I remind you, this is not a criticism. It is a statement of fact. The transition to this posture took place over the mid-1950s and early-to-mid-1960s. It was the beginning of the end for Customer care as a way of life; and, to a very large extent, for the kind of salesperson who put foremost the relationship he created with the Customer, and put the selling second.

Kotler went on to point out that the selling mentality requires that:

● You think in terms of sales volume.

● You think in the short term (next sale).

● You think in terms of individual Customers rather than the market as a whole.

● You think fieldwork is more important than desk work.

(On hearing the last one, one weary, worldly-wise sales director called out from an audience – 'Not on expenses day!' We know how he feels!)

Whether Professor Kotler had an academic, crystal-ball-like mentality, or whether the US got there first, we can speculate. Certainly, to many nations, US methods became the role-models of the quantity-selling age. Or were they just a little more extreme than others?

Now the time has come for salespeople to look at the new challenge: to examine the ways of the past 30 years and to decide how they can maintain the quantity but develop methods that do not leave devastation and a trail of bodies behind them. This is not as hard as it seems. There are improved communications, data-bases and all manner of aids becoming available to assist. But the sales director, the John Wayne-like, charismatic superhero who led his salesforce like some cavalier hit squad, is well on his way out.

The shift in selling style warrants much greater attention, and it shall have it: the whole of Chapter 16 where we look at my three generations of selling and identify just how the style has to change and what influences have brought all this about. Meanwhile, this short, introductory chapter has served to identify the changes going on in selling as one of the key factors in the next decade and to show that:

- Selling is not a Customer-driven process. It is a production-driven process.

- Selling requires that the market be manipulated and exploited to achieve its aims.

- Selling, has, sadly, become a process which is overinfluenced by the quantity obsession, and thus shorter-term objectives have won out over longer-term objectives; the sale has taken precedence over the Customer relationship. In effect, this means the second sale has lost out to the first!

8

The Rise of Marketing Ideas

Northwestern University has a distinguished record in leading edge thinking and teaching in marketing; and two very distinguished professors have played a huge part in creating that reputation. One of those professors is Phil Kotler, a man whose work, of some 15 years ago, is now beginning to look almost prophetic (he shares this distinction with another prophet, Ted Levett). The second professor is Louis Stern, of whom more will be said in a moment. Meanwhile let's revisit Kotler's article 'From Sales Obsession to Marketing Effectiveness', as published in the *Harvard Business Review* and see what he suggests is the object of marketing. He wrote: 'Marketing focuses on the needs of the buyer. It is preoccupied with how to generate Customer satisfaction at a profit.' This is theoretically correct. However, sadly, since Kotler wrote that in the late 1970s, many years have passed, and the pendulum that I believe he was trying to stop swinging even further towards its quantity climax, continued regardless for a further 20 years. Now he will see it on the way back and, thus, like someone with a broken watch, will have the pleasure of being right twice.

Kotler further explained that the tasks of the marketer are very different from those of the seller. He proposed that they:

- think in terms of long-term trends, threats and opportunities;

- think in terms of Customer types and market segment differences;

- think in terms of developing good systems for market analysis, planning and control.

The route and path of the changes

Yet marketing has as much change to make as selling. I mentioned at the beginning of this chapter, Professor Louis W Stern, a colleague of Professor Kotler, also 'carrying on the Northwestern tradition', as he once described it to me. I have twice seen Lou

Stern make a similar presentation – once in Cannes at a strategic symposium and once much, much further afield when we found ourselves grappling with our consciences (and most pleasantly surprised, at least by the marketing community) in Johannesburg, South Africa. Lou and I had been booked for the same conference. He had the honour of the keynote opener; it was more of an eye opener.

The last 30 years predicts the next ... how many?

Lou Stern presented an analysis of marketing over the last 30 years which he and Phil Kotler had worked on together and their resulting predictions, based on this, for 'at least the next ten'.

When you look at the tables Lou kindly sent to me for Marketing 2000, you can see quite clearly where marketing is coming from and, to some extent, where it's going. The charts themselves are largely self-explanatory, but there is some background to set the perspective.

You will quickly notice a missing decade from the analysis, the 1970s. Professors Kotler and Stern discerned that there were so many distorting factors in the 1970s that it skewed the picture future. See if you agree. Certainly, some of the factors they list hold fairly painful memories for me. In the UK, along with their list, we had three-day working weeks, crippling power strikes, and terrible political and union unrest undermining our commercial scene and playing havoc with our export performance.

> *What happened in the 1970s*
> 1. unexpected cost inflation;
> 2. shortages of needed materials;
> 3. new technological breakthroughs;
> 4. unwanted government regulations;
> 5. high interest costs;
> 6. aggressive internal competition;
> 7. the end of the baby boom;
> 8. unemployment.

Phil Kotler and Lou Stern's look at the decades of marketing fell under three main headings and are tabulated here as Tables 8.1, 8.2 and 8.3 and covering the 1960s, 1980s and 1990s.

Let me show you what I mean by a clear route and path. Take a look at line 1 of Table 8.1. Mass marketing evolves to segmented marketing, which evolves to niche and customised marketing.

Table 8.1: Product/market strategies

1960s	1980s	1990s
Mass marketing & product differentiation	Segmented marketing & product proliferation	Niche and customised marketing & product positioning
Product orientation	Market orientation	Customer/ competitor/channel orientation
Random product lines and products	Full product lines	Product line rationalisation
Growth mission for all products	Differentiated mission for each product	Strategic mission for each product
Random market coverage	Maximum market coverage	Selective market coverage
Domestic marketing	Multinational marketing	Global marketing
Standardised marketing	Regional marketing	Local marketing

Take that back to Chapter 2, and you'll see how this progression relates to what marketing services and technology were delivering. This included mass mailings through to the almost individualised mailings that current technocreativity facilitates.

Setting the scene for the future

A prerequisite of 'total quality marketing' is that it establishes relationships before or during the sales process. And then it continues to recognise that, given the level of product quality, of course, ongoing sales will prosper so long as the relationship is satisfactory, poor sales often being one of the more obvious results of a poor relationship.

What we need to look at, to enjoy the true predictive value of both Stern's and Kotler's conclusions, is a correlation of some of the factors and their value and contribution to the building of relationships. So, assuming that you have absorbed the left to right

Table 8.2: Marketing mix strategies

1960s	1980s	1990s
Survey research	Qualitative research	Decision support system research
Competing on product features	Competing on price lines and price	Competing on quality, design, and service
Pricing based on cost	Pricing based on competition	Pricing based on Customer perceived value
Suppliers/distributors as adversaries	Suppliers/distributors as cost-centers	Suppliers/distributors as partners
Generalised sales force	Differentiated sales forces	Multiplexed sales force
Hard selling and heavy advertising	Heavy sales promotion	Targeted and coordinated communications

Table 8.3: Corporate strategies

1960s	1980s	1990s
Core business development	Conglomerate diversification	Synergistic diversification
Cost excellence	Strategic excellence	Implementation excellence
Scale economies	Experience economies	Economies of scope
Hierarchies	Markets	Governance structures
Autonomous corporation	Mergers and acquisitions	Strategic alliances
Independent marketing functions	Coordinated marketing functions	Coordinated business functions

lines of the three tables, let us now piece together some of the items from the top to bottom of the right-hand column. From this you can see just how many of the items from the 1990s column endorse, facilitate or suggest the building of relationships and an individualised approach to marketing. From this the direction of marketing progress is quite clear. We are going backwards to the future. The quality elements that have been driven out over time by the quantity merchants are about to be put back again. The marketer's biggest problem will be to find the tenacity and perseverance to hold out for the long-term benefits that will surely accrue, and to find the funding to pay for it all. In fact, let's take each of the contributory points and look at it briefly:

Niche and customised marketing and product positioning

Marketing is lining itself up to deal with smaller and smaller units. Much of the business-to-business market has accepted individualisation for some time now. Plainly, this is a posture aimed at the long-term relationship to make all that customisation worthwhile and profitable. It is coming to the consumer markets.

Customer/competitor/channel orientation

Look how specific your marketing has to become, no longer satisfied with what the consumer wants and thinks, now you must react to Customer types, relate each of those to the relevant competitors and channels, and act accordingly. This makes strategy much more complex and tactics quite diffuse.

Product line rationalisation

You're rationalising the product line so that it makes more sense to the Customer. This enables more and more marketers to plan the way the relationship should develop – and to encourage Customers along that path by more readily being able to offer the right product at the right time. Again, this is quite clearly a relationship facilitator.

Strategic mission for each product

This takes forward the cause of the last point; that is, that a clear path is laid down – not the same path for all, but a clear path for each – and that each product within the rationalised line has a mission in the growth and cultivation of the relationship.

Selective market coverage

We've already looked at the ways many of the media are beginning to address this new highly targeted objective of the marketer. As the media rates increase in terms of the numbers they deliver for the cost, so the need for fine tuning and cutting wastage to a minimum increases proportionately.

Global marketing/local marketing

I have lumped the last two together. Although an apparent paradox, the riddle is solved by the saying that has become popular 'Think global, act local'. It says it all in this context too!

Competing on quality, design and service

Notice the absence of price! Not an actual absence, of course, but a recognition of an experience many have shared that the more individually tailored the product or service, the more value it has to the individual for whom it has been created, and therefore – all things being equal – the more it is worth. However, this point holds the clue that Customers who have or are beginning a relationship will look more and more at the quality you deliver, since they have in prospect a longer term. They will look at the design capabilities you have; the promise that the next product will meet their needs further or deeper; and the service you give. Get these right and you're worth your weight in gold! And, importantly, you are far more difficult to compete with. Any fool can compete on price. In the past, too many of them have.

Pricing based on Customer-perceived value

As the proud owner of a completely priceless (to me) BMW, its mileage well over 110,000 and me too attached to part with it, I asked a dealer, 'What's it worth?' He smiled rather condescendingly, left his price guide firmly in his pocket, and said, 'What you can get for it!'

For the future, marketing will find itself enjoying the same thought, but for the reasons we have already looked at. The more the quality, design and service aspects are addressed and the more individually tailored the product, then also the higher the price perception – and the price obtained. Thus, happily, we can see that as Customers get more demanding, they will be prepared to pay more for their improved goods and services. So here, then, the marketer will find some of the funding for his investments in the longer term, using total quality marketing.

Suppliers/distributors as partners

Over the next decade, there will be a major shift in the custody of the relationship. We will need to discuss this point, and although I would like to share my view and, to some extent, my advice with you, it is possible you may find it controversial. Thus, it will follow after this run-through.

Lou Stern's point is – particularly in the business arena and, I guess, the personal-services consumer arena – that the role of the distributor, dealer or intermediary (often almost an adversary in the past) will reposition to become much closer and more co-operative.

Multiplexed salesforce

The FMCG companies popularised the use of brand or speciality salesforces. Thus one buyer might have two or three salespeople dealing with him – one for each brand or group of brands. Each had a different view of him, each dealt with him differently. Not one of them looked at his total spend with the company. Some called personally, some dealt by phone, others were van sales. The buyer became confused and undervalued.

Cast your mind back to the notion of total communications management. This proposes that one person controls the communications and therefore looks after and understands the situation with any given Customer at any given time. For this to work, clearly, this person must represent all the company brands and products or services. Such persons may need the help of specialists to support them, but, in essence, they are multiplexed. Their mission is to understand and communicate how best the Customer can benefit from the full range of products or services on offer. You can see why, from this explanation, so many companies relegate the brand almost to a recognition device and seek to transfer or extend the loyalty to the corporation. Hence my development of the phrase, the brand behind the brand.

Targeted and co-ordinated communications

This joins together the need to target, thereby maximising spend, reducing wastage and focusing the message with the co-ordination and understanding of total communications management.

Implementation excellence

At the end of the day, no marketing can move inferior products. Many of the world's leading manufacturers have moved on from excellence. Indeed, I have been suggesting for some time that Peters and Waterman should get together again to write *In Search of Absolute Bloody Perfection*. IBM would buy a copy. Its latest quality-improvement programme, Six Sigma, has the intention of improving the company's excellence level over a four-year span by a factor of 20,000 to accept no more than 3–4 defects per million units. Perfection has become the avowed goal of many forward-thinking companies. Apart from the human interaction within the relationship, there is nothing other than product perfection that can foster such close accord. However, by the new millennium, expectation of product perfection will be so high that almost everything will actually focus on the relationship and the individuals that make it happen. More evidence that we're going backwards to the future!

Strategic alliances

The shift in corporate strategies to encourage alliances is yet another sign that the real products of tomorrow are information and knowledge. The alliances are about knowing which to buy, to a degree, but more, how to use them or what to use them for. I have already presented Marketing 2000 a number of times for software houses who have held symposia for their Clients and prospects which were co-sponsored either by other partner software houses or by computer manufacturers whose aim was to sell the boxes which processed the data using the software. This kind of *ad hoc* co-operation will become more formalised (as we discussed in Chapter 3) in relation to the need for smaller companies to compete on the international global markets.

Co-ordinated business functions

I have often thought that marketers can be quite an insular-minded group. We are often quite ready to tell the world (or our market) what it thinks – or what it should think – and, equally arrogantly, to pass this information on to our colleagues in production or planning. After all, we know what's right, because we're in touch with the market. Ironically, we have demonstrated over the last two decades at least that we are actually very bad at listening to the Customer. We seem often to hear but not necessarily to listen. The marketing world is full of marketing directors who take the views, strategies and policies of the company to the market or the Customer, but sadly devoid of marketing directors who accept the duality of their responsibility and fully represent the market to the company. And there are even fewer still who, as board members, can see that aspect of their task which is to be the voice of the Customer on the board.

Marketing people must take on much wider skills, or become, at least, much more aware of them. Marketing is not an insular or isolated function, and for the future it will be even less so. Marketing will become even more integrated into the very fabric of the business. Therefore, it is essential that marketing people become more rounded business people. This is a need which our academies and syllabus controllers must address and quickly.

I hope you will see by now the valuable job Professors Kotler and Stern's analysis has done in defining the trends for marketing through the next decade and more. I have related some of their points to highlight the terrific, almost magnetic, pull of so many of them towards the relationship as the centre of all we do in marketing for the future. However, I have left two points which I want to look at – the first is the subject of the role of the intermediary – wholesaler, retailer, dealer, distributor, etc; and the second is the increasing need to look behind the brand and increase activity to add power to corporate image and positioning.

Whose brand is it anyway?

In Western Europe, I do think we are going to have to see a regaining of control by a lot of brand owners. For, in certain areas the strength of the brand has almost been hijacked or perhaps neutralised by some of the larger specialist retailers. This story was first told in my last book, and the situation has worsened since I reported the story of my conversation with the marketing manager of a white-goods manufacturer – in fact, a refrigerator maker – who, as I was given to understand, in effect, waited to be told by certain large retailers, firstly, whether he would get any floor space at all; secondly, how many units of what types the retailers would take; and, thirdly, what price they would pay for them. These particular retailers – and others like them – controlled sufficient outlets to be able to dictate terms this way.

This same problem reared its head again when I carried out a small, in-house programme for one of Europe's leading names in the small electrical goods field. The first problem we hit at the start of the day was that the company had lost control of its margin and now, effectively, was dictated to by the majors in their market. Naturally, this power was used to squeeze the company (which had brand leadership in several areas) to cut its margin to the bone. The result, of course, was that the retail groups were now acting so greedily and so short-sightedly that the company was facing understandable difficulties in maintaining its investment in quality, Customer service and new product development.

The short answer is there is no short answer

The next few lines are not a prediction; they are a hope. A hope that, as we move towards times of increased quality, we will see a resurgence of the time-honoured values in retailing. Let's think about these.

Essentially, it seems to me, there are two types of brand with which retailers must deal. The first is the brand which the Customer will buy anyway – soapflakes in the supermarket are as good an example as any. Here the retailer really has only two major decisions to make. Whether to stock, and if so, whether and how to promote. I would call this latter the promotional influence. Such products are usually simple commodities essentially requiring, as far as the brand holder is concerned, the optimum shelf space, and, as far as the Customer is concerned, a fair price and reasonable circumstances in which to buy. Simplistically, the market for such products is created by the product's performance at meeting the needs or expectations of its buyer, and by the efforts of the manufacturer in spreading the gospel through the usual marketing methods. The retailer in this example is, to use a good, old-fashioned word, a purveyor. The only real complication in this process is where the store-owner, chain or buying group offers its own-brand alternative. The practice originated as a low-price alternative, but it has matured to a point where, to bring back the UK's Tesco for an encore, Tesco can use its own brands to further its Green moves by offering higher-priced but Greener or organic alternatives. Others have followed suit.

By and large, and to differing degrees of sophistication, this process has a sense of equilibrium. The manufacturers provide the product and the demand (brand demand and loyalty); the retailers provide the arena – and often have a hand in providing their share of the demand. So that is the promotional brand.

Then there is the second type of brand which I shall refer to as the broker brand. Here the retailers provide more than just the arena. They provide (or should!) a range of choices, value for money, and service. And lastly, they provide two additional items: expertise and advice.

Here again the retailer is charged with providing what I described earlier as the arena and all that goes with it; but equally, here he becomes the 'honest broker' as far as the Customer is concerned – providing advice to match the right product(s) or service(s) to the particular Customer. He also provides expertise, most frequently in terms of after-sales support to the Customer – and possibly further sales where supplies and consumables are involved. I call this retailer the 'honest broker' since in my idealistic account here, he is deemed to be that by – significantly – both the brand owner and the buyer of the brand.

When this balance is distorted – for example, the manufacturer interferes to the detriment of the retailer (or lets him down) – they both suffer. The Customer buys another brand from another retailer. Essentially, here the retailer has to purvey the product and act as custodian of the goodwill that the brand owner has built up – often with the invaluable support of his retailers – in the brand.

In my view, retailers who deal in 'honest broker' products should accept the limitations of their role and the responsibilities that go with it. Once they try to dictate, as opposed to apply sensible negotiatory pressure for the Customer's best interest, they have stepped beyond their remit and become an intolerable interference which potentially has drastically detrimental effects on the consumer's position in the long term. To those involved in marketing such products and those who have lost control there is no short or easy answer. The only way to restore power is long, risky and expensive. In many cases the damage will have taken place over five or even ten years, and to minimise the risk could take as long. It is my belief that you must do it to survive in a world of increasing quality and Customer service levels. Margins should increase over the following years as value perceptions increase and as Customers become more demanding. It is essential that you start right now the battle to control margins where they have been lost. Otherwise, as the cycle of product development and the life span of the new products developed decreases, you will be sucked into a vortex of decline so strong you will not survive.

The new power of corporate image

As the marketing mix reshuffles itself to cope with the future, each of the voices of its disciplines is claiming that it has an increased role in the future. Sales promotion is a fine example in which the practitioners are making all manner of new claims for their trade and effectively digging themselves into an entrenched position which has far more to do with the old ways of exploitation selling than it has to do with satisfaction marketing. However, I know there are some among their ranks who can and will make this change. And they will reap the rewards they deserve.

I think that the only mistake in listening to the voices of the disciplines would be to take any strategic notice of them. Just whom you should be listening to will be revealed in Chapter 14. In the meantime, one of those voices can be heard crying out that it shall have increasing prominence – and it is right. It is the voice of the corporate identity, or, as I have referred to it several times, 'the brand behind the brand'.

The hard fact is that we face an epoch where there is a convergence of factors over which an organisation's failure to address its corporate image and position will seriously damage its health. These factors include parity products, both better and more similar, and consumers who are more informed, more vocal, more sophisticated, more demanding and more willing to vote with their cash.

I remember Murray Raphel reminding me that people often bestow human qualities on the companies they deal with. 'Just listen to the way they describe them', he explained, 'they say they're a mean outfit. Or pretty generous types. Or friendly. Or standoffish. These are not corporate qualities; these are the qualities or failings of another human being.' He's right! And so, in a way, it is fair to suggest that a corporate identity is an expression of corporate personality.

Everything a company does, the way it acts, the opinions it expresses, and the people it hires, as well as the way it treats its Customers, is seen, to a lesser or greater degree, as an expression of that personality. Thus, the identity can be used quite powerfully to join with, differentiate from, or simply endorse a chosen position. I am suggesting for the future that, as the products get more similar, the corporate identity should support and enhance the role of the brands. Naturally, the methods used to do this will vary depending on which of the three classic identities the business has adopted. These are:

- The monolith – an organisation that centres its whole style on one strong core name and visual presentation, eg IBM and BMW.

- The patron – this company operates through a series of brands, often having no logical relationship to each other or to the organisation. Often, too, they have been added through acquisition or merger. Nestlé and Proctor & Gamble are examples.

- The umbrella – a cluster organisation which endorses or sponsors multiple activities – eg General Motors.

In this chapter we have covered a lot of ground, much of it difficult to include comprehensively in a short summary, but here is an attempt:

- Whereas the old-fashioned sales techniques are on the decline, marketing techniques are on the increase. Much of this softer, more professional style has to do with the longer-term objectives that result.

- When you consider the essential qualities that Professor Louis Stern predicted for the 1990s, an incredible 14 out of 17 had to do with, or would facilitate the growth of, long-term, broad-based relationships; the same relationships that are the cornerstone of total quality marketing.

- The correlation of these factors demonstrates clearly that the future lies in the past. The ways of quantity must now give way to those of quality.

- Many companies, in their conviction that quality holds the future, have moved on from the pursuit of excellence to the pursuit of perfection.

- Marketing people must show far greater awareness of broader business skills and acquire broader knowledge in this respect.

- Marketing leaders must pay greater attention to their responsibility as the voice of the Customer to the board of their company.

- Brand owners would be well advised to stay in control of their brands, particularly in relation to margin, from which so much else in the future will require investment, particularly Customer service, product development and brand and corporate strengthening. Those who have lost control of such factors should start the battle to regain it now.

- Retail groups who step beyond their remit as the purveyor and/ or 'honest broker' and seek to exert undue influence on manufacturers' margins do so in the knowledge that, at the end of the day, it is against their Customers' best long-term interest.

- In the battle to differentiate choices in a market of increasingly similar products, corporate identity will play an increasing part, underlining the point made earlier.

9

The New Demands of the Customer

There seems to be hordes of people who involve themselves in Customer-care tactics, and very few in strategy. This is a great shame. For Customer care – to provide anything like the levels required for relationship-centred total quality marketing – should not be thought of as a tactic. It has to be considered strategically, tactically and systematically. So many of the companies I meet talk passionately about Customer care (as they often do, incidentally, about quality) and then treat it as some kind of occasional or spasmodic campaign. Displaying a certificate in reception awarded to the person in the organisation who did something outstanding for a Customer last month is a campaign. Expecting *all* your employees to do something outstanding for a Customer every month, every week or every day suggests you've got a strategy in place.

Where doesn't the arrogance come from?

Many of the poor organisations have a reputation for attracting criticism for their failures. You have only to talk to their Customers: certain divisions of Trust House Forte, indeed certain units of Trust House Forte, for example. Barclays Bank is in danger of becoming something of a running gag in this book; Payless is another. I have a Payless story which is entirely true and which I share with conference delegates from time to time. It's good for a laugh and was originally told in a previous book. In fact, there are two excerpts that I want to take out of that book for you, and the first is the Payless story – so with grateful acknowledgement to McGraw-Hill, who published the John Fraser-Robinson Direct Marketing Series – let me take Payless first. Here's the original excerpt:

Desire is not enough – you have to make it happen

There's a branch of a well-known DIY superstore near me. I personally wouldn't work for them – simply because their name suggests you're not going to get a very fat pay packet. In fact, judging by their checkout staff, that may well be the case. My experience is that I intrude inexcusably into their day-long, apparently very important conversations with each other.

There's no contact whatsoever. However much I spend, whatever I've bought, I'm just another one in the line.

And on the rare occasions when they look up, they can never work out why I'm laughing. It's the sticker on their till that says 'SMILE – and give your Customer a nice day'.

Perhaps that promotion is over now.

Now there are two significant aspects about this story. The first is that it's obviously not just my local store that's got the problem. I know this because I've experimented around the UK and found, with some better and some worse experiences, that it is a national phenomenon. Secondly, whenever I mention this topic at a conference or seminar in the UK, the audience relate to it generally almost as one, reassuring me that it's not my being picky. In fact, I've even had the audience telling me of their own similar experiences. Obviously, this is a widespread, commonly recognised problem, not my developing a sort of commercial version of the mother-in-law joke that relies on everyone's identifying with or sharing the problem.

So, if I know about it and nearly all those I talk to know and have experienced it, what on earth is going on inside Payless HQ? Without intimate knowledge of this particular company, one can only hazard a guess. My guess is that the distance from the boardroom to the branch is about four times longer than it should be.

The second reprise from my last book is about 'my businesses'. They're few and far between, but when you come across one it's love at first sight.

Let me explain about 'my businesses'

Have you read the two Excellence books? They extol the virtues of an old-fashioned concept – that the Customer is king.

They suggest, among other philosophies, that success is assured if you dedicate yourself to Customer service. I don't have a problem with this notion. In fact, I have always tried to live up to it. It's some of the places I go to that haven't read the books!

The philosophy of 'Customer is king' requires the virtues of something we all already know. We know because we like it when it happens to us. And it's never often enough.

We all like to be remembered. We all like to be cared for. We all like recognition. We love good service and bask in personal attention.

And when you feel this happening, you have found a 'my business'. Take 'my London hotel', for example.

A few years back, I took a suite in a hotel on Park Lane. I was attending the British Direct Marketing Awards. It wasn't a good night for me. It was a great night. Probably a once in a lifetime.

I collected six or seven certificates, I think five trophies and the coveted Gold Award. For me, a real event, since it made me the only person to have received the 'Gold' twice in the entire history of the awards.

The odd bottle of champagne was seen to pass the table. But most of it stayed right there. Around 4 am I staggered into my hotel. I was showered with greetings and congratulations. There and then it seemed that everyone on night duty was joining in.

When I checked out around lunchtime I made a point of thanking the manager for his kind handwritten note which had been delivered on my breakfast tray.

Let a year pass. A year, I have to say, when I think I only used the hotel once between my 'Gold' night and today.

How do you think I felt when the front desk clerk greeted me with this:

'Mr Fraser-Robinson. We are so pleased to have you back with us again. We checked with your secretary, and she said it was Awards night. So we've given you the same suite as last year. It seemed so lucky for you.'

And more along those lines.

How did I feel? Wouldn't you make that 'my hotel'?

So what is this? Salesmanship? Professionalism? Excellence?

Yes, it is undoubtedly all those things. It's also notetaking, record-keeping, and a great deal of belief in the very highest standards of relationships.

Have you noticed how people shower accolades on professionals? You go to the grocer. You go to the supermarket. But you talk about 'my accountant', 'my solicitor'. Even the ones you don't like. 'My bank manager'. You decide to 'own' these people because they are important to you. Or, rather, because they've made themselves important to you, or even influential in your life.

So I know I've made it when a Client says, 'JFR is my marketing man!' – I still have a job to do when they say, 'I use JFR'. Personally, I 'use' a toilet.

My advice is to go for a 'my' position in the lives of your Customers. No matter whether you're a (my) charity, a (my) jeweller or a (my) supermarket. They owe you when they own you. Because you've made yourself theirs.

There's nothing particularly new in this thought. Pendulums swing. And this one is on its way back.

Maybe you have a favourite good service story, or perhaps a place where you always feel special, or even welcome. Perhaps you have places you go where you're recognised and made a fuss of. If you're typical, you'll react by going there regularly, taking your friends, and generally giving them a terrific 'word of mouth' testimonial whenever you get the opportunity.

I have always described word of mouth as the cheapest, most effective kind of advertising you can buy: the trouble is, of course, you can't buy it. You have to earn it.

I maintain, and I know that I am among many who feel this way, that we are going to see all this change radically. In the same way that the bushfire of democracy was picked up in Eastern Europe, so the bushfire of 'I'm a Customer – and king is not good enough for me' will be picked up in the developed world.

Who enjoy their shopping these days?

To get a measure on how sales and marketing people feel about this, I have made a point, during all my Marketing 2000 conferences, of asking audiences, 'Hands up. Who enjoys going to the Supermarket?' There are some that do. In fact, if I'm honest, I do! I enjoy watching the people, and I enjoy casting a professional eye over the marketing and particularly sales promotion that is going on. But do we enjoy the shopping? My show-of-hands research tells me few people do.

Back to Barclays Bank again! While writing parts of this book I spent some time in the town of Weymouth in Dorset. The Barclays branch there has 'streamlined' itself to have perhaps a dozen cashiers or tellers and, of course, two personal bankers! I decided to visit during a lunch hour and found myself among a queue of some 30 or more people, waiting like good citizens to have the honour of a cashier's attention for a short spell. Barclays Weymouth branch is well organised. If you visit during the lunch hour, of course, half the cashiers are at lunch. Thus, the management team there have thoughtfully installed a Q-matic This ingenious device tells you, when you are lucky enough to get to the front, which of the cashiers not at lunch will pass the time of day with you. To celebrate this golden moment, it chimes like a slightly damaged doorbell. As I waited with the other Customers, many of whom, like half the cashiers, were in their lunch break, it became quite obvious that the system the management had devised worked extremely well for the bank, but was the subject of some resentment and anger from their Customers. As I got to the front of the queue, I turned to face the long thin line of angry and frustrated people behind me. 'Excuse me,' I said just loudly enough to get most of their attention, 'but why do you put up with this atrocious service?' I thought I'd be a hero, chairlifted onto the shoulders of the two chaps behind me and taken on a tour of the premises while the rest of the queue followed, chanting the magic plea 'We shall, we shall soon be served.' It was not to be. Most of them looked at me, praying they wouldn't find me sitting next to them on the bus home.

So, to those nice Dorset folk and those members of my audiences who don't enjoy shopping I say again – 'Why do you put up with it?'

The answer lies in the 1960s

What has all this to do with selling? Not so much as it has to do with the mentality which now drives selling. Banking is not an experience you should enjoy; it is something you have to put up with in order to get the facility. Why is supermarketing, in the UK at least, such a joyless experience? Because we have been conditioned to accept it as such.

Although I take the UK to task particularly, I am sufficient of a European to know that the problem is in no way peculiar to the UK, but here it is certainly worse than elsewhere in Europe. In fact, it distresses me that there is much more interest in the quality aspects of marketing in continental Europe than in the UK. I, and often my wife too, take our splendid American motor home around Europe on our many conference and training trips; and we have ample opportunity to sample the various Customer-service and shopping standards throughout Europe. It may not be scientific, but it is experience! And the UK scores poorly; but it wasn't always like that.

I used to have a grocery fairy. Most British children have a tooth fairy. Me – I had this grocery fairy! The tooth fairy visits in the middle of the night and generously exchanges money for your first teeth as they are shed. My grocery fairy didn't get any teeth, but, nevertheless, generously donated a box of groceries to my mother every Friday. Miraculously, the grocery fairy always seemed to know exactly what we wanted and always called, as regular as clockwork, before Mother got me back from school each Friday.

Eventually, probably about the time my mean school friends pricked the bubble of illusion, stopping Father Christmas from conscientiously, each year, squeezing his corpulent frame, all red-faced and puffing down our chimney, I discovered the truth. It wasn't a fairy at all. You've guessed! It was a grocer. The nice man who patted my head whenever I went into his shop with Mother. The man to whom she always spent such a long time chatting about this and that. The grocer. Our grocer. He definitely ran a 'my business'.

This would be the mid-1950s. Our grocer used to ring up on a Thursday evening to discuss the weather, exchange family news, and ask Mother whether she wanted anything more than 'the usual'. Sometimes she had a list. Sometimes he prompted her. Sad to think it'll never happen like that again ...

The return of the grocery fairy (with slightly clipped wings)

What do you make of this?' said my fellow diner, waving a credit card-sized piece of plastic under my nose, with obvious pride.

'A credit card?,' I ventured.

'Nothing so ordinary,' he laughed. 'It's your Customer Visiting

Card for my supermarket. A Customer comes in, swipes it through the machine; now the store knows they're there.'

'Aha, security!' I tried again.

'Better than that. My store helps them to shop.'

The owner of this particular chain of stores went on to describe his pride and joy. As Customers enter a store, they swipe in, and the visits are logged. As they arrive at the checkout, a further swipe alerts the computer, and, as the checkout operator works through their purchases, the machine logs them and checks them against previous buying patterns. The computer then reminds each Customer of any purchases he may have forgotten based on his previous purchasing patterns. The operator keys in the products the Customer decides to take. Next the computer gives him a screen full of special offers based on what it knows he likes, and what it has in stock and on offer.

'My Customers love this service! It's just like they used to get in the old days. If they want any of the product prompts, they tell the cashier, who adds it in. By the time we've packed for them, and they're on the way out, their extra goods are waiting at the door, in a box, with their names on. On top of all that wizardry, they get a loyalty bonus that builds every time they shop here; they get express priority at the checkouts; and they get free coffee in the coffee shop. Is that good, or is that great?'

'That's great,' I agreed, my mind doing handstands at the information that his database could yield on purchase patterns, cross-brand selling, and the opportunities for phone calls just like my Mother used to get.

'What's more,' he continued, pulling back my attention, as his enthusiasm bubbled over, 'the database marketing opportunities are incredible. You know, we ring up people who've missed a visit, and offer to drop their goods round! What do you say about that?'

I looked at this happy, happy man. When you're onto a winner, it's a first, and you know you can license it round the world, it's a fabulous feeling. He looked at me, waiting for the mixture of envy, fascination and admiration which the story, no doubt, always provokes. His face took on a completely puzzled expression as I, without thinking, turned to him and replied 'You remind me of a fairy I once had.'

There's no escape – we all have to deliver

The Customer's expectation of satisfactory service, whether as a consumer or a business, is about to go through the roof. During the 1960s the quantity drive brought the benefits of mass production, competitive pricing and wider availability. Consumers who were used to postwar austerity throughout the world revelled in being able to obtain a range of goods such as they had never experienced before. Credit became more readily available and the age of plenty was well under way. In relative terms, the age of plenty has now become the age of sufficiency. Household equipment in most European countries extends to TV, refrigerator, telephone and washing machine along with many other things considered basic necessities. And that's before you step outside the home. As consumers become more experienced, they, quite justly, become more sophisticated, more aware of and concerned about their rights, and much harder to please. Why? Because they've now observed several decades of the contortions sales and marketing people will undergo in the process of obtaining their business and they know they hold the purse, so they call the tune. There is nothing wrong with this. It is right and proper they should feel this way.

Moreover, watching consumerist and pressure groups, most particularly in Europe, I am now convinced that suspicion, anger and resentment are surfacing at the processes of marketing and the people who practise it. This is all caused by the abandoning of quality, the greed of quantity-driven marketing, and the years of being subjected to exploitation-selling processes.

Now I know that, in the US particularly, selling has a very different image from that in Europe. In Australasia and South Africa, it has an image somewhere between the two. But where in the world do people implicitly trust, respect, and have total faith in sales and marketing people? Nowhere I've been. I mean, we may all be jolly nice people, easy to get on with, fun to talk with ... but trust? Whose interest do our Customers think we put first; ours or theirs? Strange really, because Mother trusted her grocer. When and why did Customers stop trusting the people who sold to them? And, the pivotal issue which determines the need for total quality marketing is how we can regain that respect and trust. The solutions to these questions are easy to identify, but more difficult to implement, as we shall learn later.

Why will the new demands of the Customer become a global issue?

The first reason is the way the media network their programmes around the globe these days. Suppose you're watching the CNN global news channel in a hotel in Copenhagen (or on cable in your sitting room at home); you're watching a newsclip of some new shopping innovation in Australia; you now want it, and you know you can have it. Your assessment of your local shops is measured against the local shops from Helsinki to Vancouver to Auckland.

Secondly, as technology and design find similar answers to the same old questions, the parity products issue forces corporations to look at other ways of securing business. Customer service, Customer care and the added-value route will turn up the heat.

Thirdly, as I have pointed out, Customers are becoming increasingly sophisticated and informed. They will, naturally, become more discerning and hold greater expectations. The only real dilemmas are not whether you should do it, whether it will do you good, or whether your Customers will like it. The dilemmas are how you will fund these new service and care levels, and what will happen to you if you don't.

I am not going into the practical aspects of Customer service or Customer-care programmes, for this is not a book about these subjects. However, it is a book about the need for them. And to practise the art of total quality marketing, you must become a master of Customer service and Customer care. For me, the building of a Customer relationship is rather like the building of a strong brick wall. The bricks are the individual sales or units of sales. The cement is the loyalty that is created in that Customer. It holds the sales process together, bonding between the individual sales, and creating strength and resilience. The water, sand and mortar from which that cement is made are Customer satisfaction, Customer service and Customer care. Total quality marketing is, in effect, a safe and secure place in which your company can weather the storms of the business world. Now you know how the walls to that safe place must be built.

Another view to which I was attracted during the processes of my research for this book was the schematic reproduced in Figure 9.1 opposite. It is stolen (with permission and my thanks) from a short book called *Sold on Service*, written by Phillip Forrest and published by the Carlson Marketing Group in the UK. Although I have some problems with the fine detail of the external marketing side,

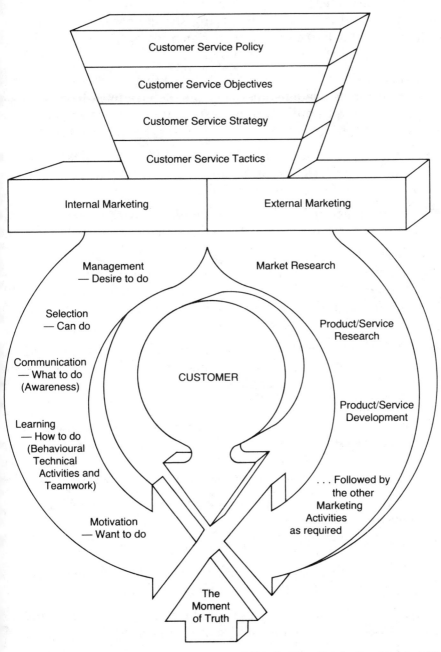

Customer Service Policy

Customer Service Objectives

Customer Service Strategy

Customer Service Tactics

Internal Marketing

External Marketing

Management
— Desire to do

Market Research

Selection
— Can do

Product/Service
Research

Communication
— What to do
(Awareness)

CUSTOMER

Learning
— How to do
(Behavioural
Technical
Activities and
Teamwork)

Product/Service
Development

. . . Followed by
the other
Marketing
Activities
as required

Motivation
— Want to do

The
Moment
of Truth

Published by Carlson Marketing Group International, UK

Figure 9.1: Internal and external marketing as vehicles for Customer service

I reproduce it here solely because the way it is designed suggests that the Customer will be almost enveloped in the two marketing processes, and this has a very caring and attentive implication.

This chapter looked at the new demands of the Customer. In it we considered the following points:

- Total quality marketing requires the building of stable and rewarding Customer relationships. Customer service must have strategic integrity and be built into the system. It must be practised by all from the top down, with no exceptions, and no excuses.

- Companies that build relationships rather than sales stand out from the crowd. They attract and receive vastly increased levels of loyalty, affection, respect and trust.

- Customer service and quality standards went into rapid and severe decline during the 1960s and 1970s. Standards throughout Europe are poor; in the UK they are markedly worse.

- An example was given in which the harnessing of technology and marketing skills was able, to a great extent, to return the quality and individual treatment to relationships, while maintaining the scale and quantities required today.

- By the end of the 1980s we had moved from the age of plenty to the age of sufficiency. The Customers have taken control of their spending. They have freedom, they have choice, and they have legs. They will use all three increasingly.

- Consumers the world over view marketing and the marketing process with suspicion and distrust. This must change, but it must be a real change. It's no good polishing our smile and our armour. We have to learn to listen and to respect, and to practise our handshake.

- The three major influences that will spread the word as far as what the Customer can get are:

    1. The media: the global village is full of gossips.

    2. Parity products: Customer service gives an attractive edge – but it's difficult to withdraw it.

    3. The Customer is more sophisticated and informed, and, as a result, more demanding and discerning.

- From a sound relationship, sales and loyalty are cultivated together. Total quality marketing uses Customer satisfaction Customer service and Customer care for the bonding process.

10

The Challenges of Changes

Has it occurred to you that marketing is in a rut? Think about it! Look at how little has changed in the last 30 years. Don't look at the fine detail; the proliferation of television advertising, the transformation from corner store to hypermarket, or the increase of wealth and the rise of the wasteful, materialistic society. Look at the fundamental process and structure of your business – whether it be in selling, advertising or marketing.

You agree? It's in a rut. Nothing of any real consequence to the process has changed at all. Our information systems are better; the disciplines argue more aggressively with each other, making strategic planning increasingly more confusing. Yet the good old marketing department looks pretty much as it always did; nobody can quite decide where PR fits, the market information still comes in on hard copy, and the agency still overrates creativity and charges too much for it. So what's new?

As we move into the next millennium, companies will have to deal with more change and do it faster than ever before. It is well forecast; the mass of companies involved at every stage of preparation are written about and talked about in almost every book, magazine and conference. Some are studying to decide what to do; some have decided and are setting off; some, like SAS, IBM, British Airways and many more, are well down the road. Where are you? Not your company, your marketing department or team. The fact is, marketing will see more change than all the other business functions. It's change[3]. The change within marketing and the change within the market would be change[2]. When you multiply again by the change within your company, then it's change to the power of three.

One rarely thinks of marketing people as a group without perception or vision, and yet (no doubt a version of the cobbler's shoes syndrome) I find very little concentration on or preoccupation with the factors that matter for the times ahead. Let's do some of that now. In fact, both this chapter and the following (on new workplaces) will look at areas that marketing, advertising and sales people have been somewhat negligent in exploring.

So where will all this change come from? And what types of change should we expect?

Identifying the pressures

I think we have already identified the first of the major pressures for change, the need to stay flexible. As I suggested earlier, this will mean a move away from the big bureaucratic marketing department of the 1970s and '80s, to the new smaller-department and bigger-budget set-up of the '90s.

The second is also something we have already unearthed, the need for marketing and technology – more precisely information technology – to get their act together.

The third area of pressure on marketing is its need to come to terms with new management styles and structures. Do not confuse this with corporate restructuring. Many companies have restructured their businesses and made the mistake of maintaining marketing as a separate specialist resource, a unit to which other departments can refer when they need, or which can pass down marketing initiatives. This may function, but it is not the most effective answer for a company that wishes to become Customer-driven or Customer-orientated. I see this as sending your army to a distant battlefield and leaving the medical corps at home. If anyone gets sick or is wounded he has to fly home to be seen to, whatever the gravity of the problem. It plainly doesn't make sense. The frontline troops need medical specialists with them at both basic and intermediate levels. The brain surgeons get to stay home.

And the fourth pressure is for marketing and particularly sales people to understand the huge difference between marketing and total quality marketing (TQM). The old sales mentality people could look on TQM as enigmatic. A fuzzy, woolly sort of business, centred as it is on the building of relationships, and, in business marketing especially, using the concept of alliances and partnerships to further its cause. The old ways are not team ways. The old ways jealously guard one's contacts and knowledge; possession is ten-tenths of the game. The future is more open in its perception of horizons, and more open in its style.

The fifth and final pressure is the need for marketing to become more responsible and to increase its understanding of business generally. We considered earlier the need for marketing people to acquire broader-based business skills. Marketing people should be business people with specialist marketing skills rather than, as hitherto, specialists in an isolated skill area. I would like to see top-level, strategic marketing skills outside the company, and most probably outside its agencies too.

These five factors, of course, are not self-contained. They have impact on each other. For example, the need to stay flexible will require better information systems and more network controls rather than departmental controls. This will make great use of the new technology available, but will require the pulling together of information technology (IT) and marketing. As marketing people acquire IT skills along with broader business skills, they may need increased specialist help, particularly on strategic matters. After all, one has only so much capacity!

Getting together with IT

This problem is out of all proportion to its solution. The solution is simple, but, as time passes, the gap widens, thus making it harder to correct. And, at the moment, marketing and IT do seem to be heading in divergent directions. Thus, the simple solution – get them together – has, over time, to cope with the greater distance between the two.

Marketing and IT seemed to part company in the 1970s, leaving probably only the slightly frowned-on direct marketers to keep up with the latest developments. Rather than backtrack in time to the point at which they parted and then start over, I prefer to build a bridge of some kind.

The most effective method so far available seems to consist of two simple steps. The first is to find and develop a common language – the 'pidgin' of your business – so the two can converse; the second is to find a common picture. This usually benefits from outside specialist help and is achieved by constructing a process diagram or flow chart of your marketing process, similar to those used by the computer people. The marketing people naturally recognise it as their process, and the computer people's eyes normally open wide with realisation of what is actually going on. This bridge-building has become very much the speciality of the Dunn Humby consultancy, whose research in this area quantified the gap so clearly.

Hitherto, IT, used to the fixed process and variable inputs of, say, the accounts department (often the reason for IT's existence), could not make any sense of the experimental, fluid, entrepreneurial and variable process (with variable inputs) of marketing. Yet this is their part of the bargain; to bring their enormous 'what if', modelling, number-crunching, information-building skills with which the new marketers can bob and weave like young boxers on an illegal substance!

So there is a short-term answer, a way to pull them back together, but in their wedded bliss, will marketing and IT require a new kind of operative? In my view, yes. And the pioneering is already being done here in manufacturing and production businesses such as Esso, Norsk Data, British Airways and BMW. These companies are looking for, encouraging and taking their part in creating what has become known as the 'hybrid manager'. This is a person who is as accomplished in IT skills as in another discipline or function. Until now, marketing has not taken IT seriously. It has only paid lip service to IT skills and done everything it could to ignore the gap rather than bridge it. Yet total quality marketing can make better use of hybrid managers than anyone else in the business.

How do you breed a hybrid?

Basically, what we are looking to achieve to bring marketing forward is a new kind of executive and manager; someone who is literate in both IT and marketing. For IT can virtually reinvent marketing. And when you look at the task of turning so many aspects of the marketing process, again particularly selling, from quantity to quality, perhaps a capability to reinvent is precisely what is needed. We need people who can take the process, step by step, examine its logic, evaluate its contribution to the building of long-term, broad-based, satisfying Customer relationships, and then reshape and remodel them to be more efficient, using the new criteria we shall consider.

A study by the British Computer Society came to the conclusion that, by the end of the 1990s, as many as 30 per cent of all managers should be hybrids. It recommended steps to create a minimum of 10,000 such managers by the middle of the decade. How many, I wonder, in marketing? Sadly, the answer will almost certainly be 'not enough', for I assess marketing's need for this new manager to be between 40–45 per cent of its total available. If the business of marketing does not forthwith start to make friends with IT, it will not begin to equip itself for the future. And no hybrid manager of any consequence will waste his value or abilities working in an environment which is not good for him or equipped for him. IT has to become established in marketing before it can maximise the benefits. Moreover, it has to show a demonstrable start at this goal before it will convince the talent it requires to be recruited.

How will the hybrid manager flourish in marketing?

Marketing departments will soon start to experience radical changes in their strategies and in their infrastructures. This new climate will be perfect for the hybrid manager. As the structure flattens out, the administrative functions and self-support services will decrease substantially. The manager in the new environment will be able to concentrate on the new quality goals, attending to the Customer-service aspects of the partnerships and allegiances which the company must form to grow and to tap new potential. And to be sure, the role of marketing in the searching out, assessing and bonding with these new partnerships is crucial. Who else can represent the Customer?

We discussed in an earlier chapter the influence of international-isation, or globalisation, as a method for large and small companies alike to find the resource for leading-edge thinking and staying ahead with technology. A further task of the hybrid will be to support the integration of sales and distribution strategies across different time and language zones and to manipulate the sophisti-cated information and communication systems this will require.

It is my experience, and this is not meant to sound patronising, that the most successful hybrids have so far resulted from line managers moving into IT rather than the other way round. IT seems to have a better reputation for performing the task than for management per se. However, it is still relatively uncommon to see senior IT people moving into other disciplines, just as, in the past, one was more used to seeing Client people moving to agencies rather than the other way. This latter situation is actually changing considerably. I suspect that, as one of the 'new' management sciences, IT has yet to acquire sufficient general business, social and political skills that it can afford to lose its best leaders.

The two qualities required of marketing's hybrid managers, will be no different from those of the hybrids at work elsewhere. These are:

1. *Experience*: current thinking suggests that 2–3 years' IT experience is required in support of the conjoint business area. With such, the manager is able to recognise the business opportunities, make a convincing case for them and sufficiently anticipate the practical implementation issues.

2. *Skills*: hybrids need to make a feature of their interpersonal, social and presentation skills. It is these which enable them to overcome the classic objections to IT projects. With accomplished social, political and organisational skills, the hybrid can command green lights right down the block.

Esso in the UK has been one of the most rapid and successful companies at identifying the advantages of hybrids and then cultivating them. By the beginning of the decade, Esso had consciously placed some of its best IT managers in line positions, successfully bucking the directional trend. Equally, Esso looked to fill senior IT posts with business managers from other areas; effectively, thereby, it 'grew' its own hybrids. Esso believes this to be responsible for an increase from 60 to 90 per cent of projects delivered both on time and within budget. Marketing would revel in such a rate.

Common features which have been noted in companies where the hybrid programme is advanced suggest that they develop a bias towards strategic rather than reactive management; this, in turn, leads to greater awareness of long-term issues. Such managers flourish in open-management styles where experimentation and risk-taking are encouraged, observed and understood. For marketers who are thinking of 'crossing the line', it is not necessary to develop more than an empathy and understanding for the role of technology; deep technical skills are rarely required. However, such individuals will need a strong sense of purpose, the ability to deal with high stress levels, and the faith of a bridge-builder – not just knowing that you can get to the other side and back again. In the drive to build effectiveness with marketing departments, groups and teams, I believe hybrids to be in a fine position to acquire leadership positions since they should be ideally skilled to provide a solid sense of direction; to create teamwork and engender the spirit required to encourage this; and lastly, to inspire, encourage and practise truly creative thinking.

The new styles of management in marketing

Perhaps the first and most noticeable change will be the new, broader vision of tomorrow's marketer: more the business person, less the obsessive marketer. There will also be an even greater consciousness that to serve the Customer perfectly, the whole organisation needs to be fit and healthy. At times this need to balance the corporate good in the welfare of all Customers against the specific service requirements of one or a group of Customers may prove something of a dilemma for this 'new' marketer. At the end of the day, however, it will prove that the corporate good serves all Customers.

But a word of warning goes with this. Some years ago, as a director of three inter-trading companies within a group, I introduced a series of team meetings. However, in order to break down the formal structures and encourage cross-boundary dialogues, the teams were formed of the people who dealt with each other day to day, rather than those who worked in the same department as each other. Thus, for example, drivers got to talk to the people who prepared their loads, and both of those to the people who took the phone calls that specified the load. It was difficult not to include the switchboard operators in every team! These were monthly meetings; they lasted as long as they lasted, and the aim was that half the time would be in 'company time' and half would be in 'personal time'.

The meetings started with a designated leader, but became democratic. This move sounded right, but, in fact, it left me undecided about the better of the two. Often a sensitively and thoughtfully designated team leader worked better than the democrat type. Although there was no rank, it took courage for even the most lucid and articulate young secretary to face up to a director ... and as you may judge from the comment, as much strength and personal security from the director to forget his or her rank altogether. It started well. The basic premise behind all meetings was that you could raise any topic you liked as long as there was a clear implication that the Customer would benefit in the end. Thus, for example, staff welfare had a clear mandate – discontented staff don't work at their best! Gradually, however, at the team leaders' forum, where the actions were decided and judgements were made, we found the items raised went from enthusiastic and outward thinking to enthusiastic and a great deal more inward thinking. At times, the approved link for getting your item on the agenda, the one that had to do with staff welfare being in the Customer's best long-term interest, was stretched to extraordinarily new and ingeniously creative lengths. It was also interesting to watch the qualities and moods of one company cross the boundary and spread to another.

Overall, the experience was beneficial, worthwhile and quite fascinating to observe. I certainly wouldn't hesitate to use it again in appropriate cicumstances. The proviso is that one may need to monitor and assist until those who are not used to freedom and democracy learn to use them fully, and those who are used to power and command learn to control themselves and enjoy the sight of others exercising their freedom of opinion. The experience, I believe, did most to make me explore concepts of less hierarchical, more democratic management, as well as the use of teams which in themselves had formal recognition in the corporate structure and which benefited from strong, visionary and creative leadership. These teams learned to talk to each other all the time rather than at scheduled meetings.

My point here can be further illustrated by perhaps an unkind but factual observation. Many countries enjoy the existence of 'mutual' insurance companies. They often have some special status, having no shareholders and therefore existing (it is claimed) entirely for the mutual benefit of their policyholders. The added edge is that profits, instead of being distributed to the shareholders, are returned to the benefit of the policyholders, thereby increasing their returns, keeping prices to the minimum or adding value to their cover or ancillary services. It is quite noticeable that accommodation, staff facilities, and conditions and terms of employment in such companies are generally well at the top end of their business! I guess balancing the welfare of the company against the welfare of the Customer works well as long as enthusiasm, motivation and commitment stay strong and pure, a condition which has to do with leadership.

Certainly, our 'all-rounder' style of manager should have far better leadership credentials. Interestingly, it was reported that at BMW, managers are encouraged to enshrine the best attributes of each of the three different kinds of manager they had identified:

1. the specialist or expert;

2. the leader who pulls his team together;

3. the skilled and corporate game player who is capable of recognising and using power within the organisation.

No one single style of manager, they claim, was better than another; however, it was noted that as you rose in rank so the last-named, the game player, became more important. Some things never change!

Who would you like to work with and where?

As we move into the next century, we have arrived at a point where, compared with the last century, we have a significant change. We used to have to move the people to the work. For a vast number of businesses, this will not be the case in the future. They can move the work to the people.

This may prove a huge temptation for many non-production-based companies. Why, for example, should a finance house or insurance company pull workers in to do their work when so much of it could be done from home with the simple provision of some basic communications equipment? To focus on this aspect solely from the marketing point of view, and to look at the right probability from your organisation's point of view, you must look at the element of team influence, and, particularly bearing in mind the degree of social interchange in the marketing business, consider all aspects of this team mentality, not least team spirit. Further, you might consider the likelihood that teamwork will become more vital for successful total quality marketing. The major question is, who will be in the team with the marketer – fellow marketers or, more likely, as I propose, mostly others from other areas. This brings us to two final challenges of change: the rise of the team and, therefore, the increased emphasis on leadership.

The rise of the team

Teams have existed in marketing and sales for decades. What is a product group if not a team? Has the sales director not been welding his salesforce together as a team for years (it's a pity his reward system often turns them against each other!); hasn't the sales promotion unit been a good team? Yes, yes, yes. But it's the type of team they are. Some, so built into the marketing hierarchy they're as essential as the leg of a tripod; others clinging to the infrastructure like benign parasites.

You could look at advertising agencies and claim they have been organised into teams since they began. Is there not an account-handling team, a creative team, a traffic team, a planning team, a media team?

Teams in marketing will change to show the two types in place: first, a formal multidiscipline team. This will be a part of, either a network structure, or a broadside structure, as discussed in Chapter 20. Depending on the complexity of their marketing task, these teams will themselves fall into two categories: the autonomous business unit, where marketing is but one function of the team; or, where the problem is more complex, the specialist marketing team which includes a whole, full-capability marketing group. Where the formal team is not appropriate, marketing leaders will recruit special project task forces – superteams, if you will – to investigate, shape and manage the special tasks which occur or which are created.

Similarly, agencies, themselves concerned about both the relationships they build and the relationships of which they are, in effect, guardians for their Clients, will choose to work in multidiscipline teams. Headed by a business controller, they will, in effect, become microagencies glorying in furthering the corporate cause, but as self-run, self-sufficient, wholly free, total businesses. They may look after just one or two or three Clients. Their location is open to their choice! Even central resources, of which, I suspect there may only be one – information – will be networked. This lean, lithe, super-energy unit will come as a huge culture shock to the old timers of advertising who have been so brainwashed by their business as to view the size of their corporate edifice, the depth and thickness of their carpet pile, the length of the board-room table, or the style and design of their office to be as much a show of their own corporate ability as it is the work-based girdle that holds their own sense of self-accomplishment and self-worth together.

It is said that teams work best where a task or series of tasks depend on three or more people and/or disciplines. Usually marketing does. And the more complex the work, often the more suited it is to teams. Total quality marketing will benefit, without doubt, from team methods. It will benefit from the cross-disciplined attitude that enables and encourages breakthrough-style thinking and problem solving, and from teams on both sides – agency and Client – that are strong enough to make their own decisions: the more autonomous the better. Marketing that requires quality cannot succeed in the tunnel-function world where each discipline must be briefed, enthused and motivated, and then controlled and overseen until the whole series of tasks that makes the project is successful. It needs teams drawn up that care about, and whose motivation is centred on, the whole project, thus breeding a group commitment to the business objective. Inevitably, the spirit with which the team dedicates itself will turn the spotlight on the leader and his or her leadership skills.

Lead from the middle

As marketing sheds or flattens its hierarchies and cultivates its new, smaller microagencies within agencies, so too, its workers will have to come to terms with new styles and situations. I prefer to envision this as a series of circles, with the centre bull's-eye as the leader, and variable size pie sections as the disciplines, the proportion of the pie slice being the proportion of influence of the discipline (not necessarily the number of people) (see Figure on p 190). In this environment leaders will require managers and workers who can think beyond classic hierarchies to understand and enjoy a life where power, authority or influence may not necessarily come from above, but most likely from alongside or across the circle. More and more marketing people will learn that whereas the hierarchy manager has to accept responsibility, the manager inside the team – as it were, a horizontal manager – gives out responsibility. This requires understanding of more than one discipline and adds weight to the cause of the hybrid. Just as the business of the future must learn to cope with risk and uncertainty, so must the manager who works for it. In Chapter 1 we looked at a view of this that proposed three-way marketing, on the premise that, in times of risk, long-term, satisfying relationships represented the most stable haven for the corporation. Realising this as the greatest stabilising factor for their personal security and financial welfare, total quality marketing will flourish, with the clear focus and responsibility this gives to those who work throughout TQM organisations.

The bond of friendship – the factor that makes sales a partnership

Should you be involved in consumer marketing, you might be tempted to skip this section on the reasonable assumption that it is of use only to your counterparts in business-to-business marketing.

You would be partly correct. It may be of more use to them, but far from exclusively so; service, leisure and financial consumer marketers or retailers enhancing their 'my business' or 'honest broker' positions would be well advised to consider the information.

Workers formed trade unions because these organiations harness their power; they spoke as one, but louder and stronger. NATO and the UN were formed because nations learned eventually that in a difficult, complex and uncertain world the risks are great, but not so great as when you are alone. So, too, in business, the forming of relationships on a long-term basis will breed new style partnerships and allegiances. This process is much heralded in the production and supply functions, probably because each supplier is, in turn, a Customer of another supplier! The proposal of partnership, of some kind of strategic alliance, is very often a natural goal or development of such relationships.

The most common concern about such bondings is control paranoia. That is, the fear that some kind of pressure will be exerted which will drive the company off course, or cause it to lose financial control. This fear forgets that two healthy partners make the best partnership; two content co-operators form the strongest allegiance. When the paranoia is put aside and the benefits to Customers examined, you will evaluate most alliances in their purest light. Certainly, the forming of alliances takes courage, as any relationship does. However, if you fear you may become Jonah and your partner a whale, or vice versa, neither will ever be content. The worst of all would be to enter the relationship with a victim or predator mentality. One is a dangerous psychological precondition; the other will destroy your credibility for ever. As with all relationships, an equal balance is best, but in corporate relationships there is every need to be faithful, but no need at all to be monogamous; three-, four- or five-way partnerships can work well too. If such complex inter-trading causes a problem with pricing, I urge all parties to play openly and come to terms on margins rather than prices.

Change? What change?

The kinds of change we will have to deal with has elsewhere been identified as either continuous change (you might call this the progressive development path upon which you and your business are embarked) or discontinous change (the beyond-your-control kind of change that comes from nowhere and hits where it hurts most).

Broadly, these categories suffice, with the exception that this neat pigeonholing doesn't have any cautionary ring to it – and, certainly, in relation to discontinuous change it should have. Think about it. If you're Spanish, Portuguese, Dutch or British and you're in the holiday hotel or travel business, you'll have experienced discontinuous change. It happens when you walk into work one morning and your colleague tells you the French air-traffic controllers have gone on strike again. The feeling hits your stomach like a stone. You're completely at the mercy of these ATCs. If their strike is short you suffer only a spate of cancellations; otherwise, your whole season is in jeopardy. And if you look to next year to save you and pay off the bank loan, chances are they'll do it again

Global warming is another discontinuous, unpredictable change. Having discussed this with many, many people at Marketing 2000 conferences, I'm of a mind to promote this from a discontinuous to a continuous change. Together with the greenhouse effect, it seems to have earned its place on the list of hazards, problems or opportunities which marketers need to put on their checklist of outside influences to monitor contantly. Even one charity selling limited-edition collectables to raise funds reported a major shift in consumer preferences to 'nature and natural subjects' over the last few years, with its Customers expressing strong views about the packaging materials. I contentedly report this last influence and encourage it. My heart even warmed to the UK tax collector who recently wrote to me, requesting a contribution: noticing that the reusable envelope was made of recycled paper, as was the clumsily laser-printed yet outrageous demand, I felt my resentment level drop a whole 10 per cent!

Chapter 10 was about changes. And about challenges. Some will no doubt cause you problems; they may be hard to picture and hard to believe. Others, hopefully, will excite, inspire or encourage you. Let's review the ground we covered:

● Marketing, which has seen little change of process over the last decades, is set to develop more in the next 15 years than it has since World War Two, if ...

● Marketing and IT have to get their act together, together.

● De-massifying the company infrastructure, and leaving the marketing function as a central resource, apart from distancing sales and marketing, is not the best solution for a Customer-responsive company. Marketing needs to be simultaneously near the Customer and near its own decision centre.

- Total quality marketing is an inexact science. It is an experimental, risk-taking, creative process. It deals primarily in the long term and is flexible in posture.

- Marketing people must take on new, wider responsibilities, for which they will need new skills.

- Hybrid managers, proving successful elsewhere, represent a sound and rapid method of entwining IT and marketing. However, they must develop a mutual language and a mutual picture of the process of their business. IT must see past the individual transactions; marketing must understand the logistics of its groups of transactions; both must understand the influence of the transactions – single or grouped – on the Customer relationship.

- Successful hybrid managers, for total quality marketing, will probably require two or three years' IT knowledge to complement their career marketing skills, or the reverse.

- Hybrid managers elsewhere in business have cultivated environments which should prove beneficial to marketing in the future. They are more inclined to favour strategic rather than reactive management; they flourish in open management arenas which share an appreciation of risk-taking and experimentation; they bring creative thinking – and, all in all, they could represent the most likely leaders of the next decade.

- The marketer of tomorrow has a finely tuned perception of what is good for the corporation and what is good for the Customer. And what is both.

- The 1990s will see the influence of the fact that it is becoming easier in some fields to ship work to people rather than people to work. Marketers, in evaluating this concept, must assess to what degree a team style assists their tasks, and, further, the very probable increase in such teamwork in the future of total quality marketing. The major resolution to be made is whether marketing consists of members of multidiscipline teams or remains as teams of specialists. Many fields, including advertising agencies, should study the multidiscipline team approach.

- Structural changes will require attitude changes from marketers. Greater 'horizontal' responsibilities and reporting will be observed, with a sharp decline in hierarchical behaviour and thinking.

- Trust and openness will need to be developed in many respects to encourage partnerships and allegiances. This attitude will be present in both forward and reverse marketing, both with Clients and suppliers. Greater intertrading will lead to more companies being involved in two-way traffic. Healthy partners build the best relationships, so long-term, quality issues should be foremost in the negotiations prior to co-operation. There may be safety in numbers; partnerships can be multipartnered as well as multifaceted. If price is a hurdle to marriage, negotiate on margins.

11

Our New Workplaces

It is well over a decade since Peter Drucker, the internationally lauded Professor of Social Services and Management at the Claremont Graduate School in California, predicted with unnerving accuracy the very de-massification of corporate infrastructures which is now happening all around us. Professor Drucker suggested that:

> The typical large business 20 years hence will have fewer than half the levels of management ... and no more than one-third of the managers.

The prediction proved faulty only in that it happened sooner than Professor Drucker suggested. De-massification is underway on a national and international scale. In 1990 British Telecom announced the shedding of 30,000 staff as it reduced the levels of management, a process that IBM started back in 1986. By 1989 IBM had increased the number of staff working directly with Customers by 23 per cent while expecting its US workforce to be reduced by 10,000 overall. By the end of 1989 it had reduced its payroll from 243,000 to just 206,000, a reduction of 37,000, pulling it back to its 1981 total. It launched the largest retraining and redeployment programme in its history, asking IBM staff worldwide to consider career changes and new work habits so that this massive corporate elephant could become gazelle-like in its response to Customer needs. In just three years it defied gravity and achieved:

- the retraining and reassigning of 60,000 people;
- the move of 30,000 of the above from 'overhead' positions to sales, system engineering and programming;
- a total reduction in the overhead jobs of one-fifth;
- a situation in which 50 per cent of all IBM employees now work directly in developing, making, marketing or servicing Customers' needs and solutions;
- a significant advance in its marketing force. Now over 70,000 people work with Customers. As this book goes to press, the

software development population will exceed 35,000 employees worldwide, almost 60 per cent more than four years ago.

This programme has set IBM back some $2.4 billion or $2.58 per share. The much reiterated comment by CEO John Akers (as the 1980s came to an end) was, 'We took our eye off the ball.' The IBM story, of which more later, has resulted in much praise and acclaim for IBM's remarkable achievement in turning round the company. And it is a fabulous achievement. However, it does tend to mask the lack of vision and management which let it get into such an outrageously flabby and grossly lethargic state in the first place. Taking one's eye off the ball is one thing; running a company with such extraordinary waste and underperformance is, to my mind, something altogether different; since I don't hold IBM stock, we needn't consider it further!

The death of the middle manager

Look out for your job! If you're a middle manager it could dissolve before your eyes; at least, it is in severe danger of doing so. That may not be so bad, since you may end up having much more fun, enjoying much more stimulation and getting far greater satisfaction. You'll be involved with real live Customers, getting to grips with events and actualities that really matter. It feels great. And the most significant element is that more and more people are coming into marketing, more and more people are discovering the satisfaction, pleasure and fulfilment of attending Customers' needs and desires. It is actually what business is for.

Yet there is a massive dilemma. This whole preoccupation with de-massifying companies is further confused by the de-massifying markets. Now to achieve our objectives in marketing we may have to look at fragments of fragments; niche marketing for niche markets.

Let's examine Professor Drucker's original premise and luxuriate in the benefit of hindsight. Further, let's look at the validity it holds for marketers. My confession is one of bias. In the mid-1980s I was correctly quoted as saying I would rather run a networked group of small agencies than one large one. The danger is that you set up an evolutionary continuum; no sooner have you unbundled the whole group than someone has the fabulous idea of creating a central resource for something. Then the overheads of all the different units are examined against the reduced costs of a bundled unit under one roof; the costs and facility of communications are reviewed and, surprise, yes – they too would be improved in one building. Pretty soon, you too have taken your 'eye off the ball', as IBM's Akers rather dismissively put it.

Think Customer. What's best for the Customer? For example, in the case of an ad agency, there is nothing that a small agency can't do as well as a big agency. It's generally only big for its own sake.

Look at your own business. Think Customer. Question why you are the size you are. Search for justifications. Generally there are plenty, but none to do with the Customer.

Think Customer. Examine your processes. Your systems. Your structure. Look at everything. Examine the real benefits of size. But when you look at each facet, evaluate it with those two words up front. Think Customer.

Examine the role of your people. How many touch Customers? How many exist for the benefit of the momentum of the business? How many come to work – and how many come to serve the Customers by serving the business? You'll find the more people you have who are involved with Customers, the more motivated they are. For, in today's hi-tech, automatic computerised, digital work society, every business has to become a people business. Otherwise the motivation goes. You can play computer games only for so long.

In a way it is this scenario which lies behind Drucker's thesis. So many businesses have become glorified data-processing machines. I recall in this respect those cartoons that appeared in the 1960s. They wryly poked fun at the executive who had gone to lunch only to find on return that he'd been replaced by a computer. The marginal inaccuracy was that it is whole layers of the business that are being made redundant.

If you stand back and observe businesses, you can clearly see their data processing at work. The front line gather data like scurrying ants. Often they gather more than their own weight! They return to base and pass the data to their managers. The managers sift and batch the data and pass it with a satisfied smile up to the next level. The next level devour the data hungrily. What is there here that can help the decision-making process? Finally, with decisions identified and the data processed into information, it arrives at the top ready for the decision to be made. Once that the information is considered and the decision is made, the whole process starts up once more, but in reverse. The first level down considers the decision and forms an implementation plan. The departmental or divisional responsibilities are handed down, and the news finally reaches the front line where our scurrying ant-like creatures dash frantically in and out of the marketplace, excitedly going about their business. It is a very cumbersome process.

So, when you analyse many a big corporation, and identify the tasks where size is useful, you find they are few and far between, at least when you bear in mind that as a networked group most of these benefits still exist, including the range of experience, the diverse skills of the work force, the buying power, and so on. The result of such an analysis leads to the de-massification process that Professor Drucker predicted and which many companies, like IBM, have now found leaves them in far better shape. But, importantly, the flatter structure moves the heart of the company nearer the Customer and makes the unit far more responsive to their needs. However, I maintain, for optimised marketing, reducing the hierarchy alone is not sufficient. For, at the end of the day, a hierarchy is only a mechanism to appease the fragility of man.

How does marketing relate to the de-massified infrastructures?

Marketing's major problem is that not only are the businesses it serves fragmenting, but so also is its market. It is this added factor which makes the creation of marketing as a central resource less than satisfactory. The problems are:

1. Marketing and sales become distanced (or further distanced) at a time when they need to become closer than ever.

2. Marketing as a central unit stays just as slow in response time as it always did, in contrast to the other areas which, as they speed up, will become increasingly frustrated with marketing slowness.

3. Marketing becomes less distanced from Customers, less in tune with their needs, and hence less capable of predicting the future with validity.

4. A central resource is less flexible and cannot be redeployed or refocused easily.

5. The central resource is ill-equipped and ill-positioned to join in any partnerships, allegiances or relationship building, and

will therefore not be encouraged to involve itself when, in fact, it has a vital role if success is to be achieved.

However, the greatest reason why I do not recommend marketing as a central resource is that it does not suit its role for the future. The future is not about putting on sales; it is about creating and nurturing long, healthy and happy relationships with satisfied Customers. Marketing is therefore not to be seen or used as a resource. It is, or must become, for true total quality marketing, an integral part of your product or service. Nothing less.

The argument in praise of hierarchies

Businesses – and particularly consultants – do have a habit of following trends, thus assuming that one solution suits all. There is a very lucid case for maintaining hierarchies, not the least being that they have worked well for so long. Those in favour of the status quo argue quite noisily that, in IBM's case, if Mr Akers and his team had kept their eye on the ball they wouldn't have let the company become so lethargic, flabby, indolent, and perhaps even a little arrogant.

The most vocal of academics in favour of hierarchy is the US professor, Elliot Jacques, whose book *Requisite Organisation: The CEO's Guide to Creative Structure and Leadership* (Casson Hall/ Gower, 1989) lands firmly on the side of hierarchies for large companies. The only thing wrong with hierarchies, the professor suggests, is that after some 3000 years we haven't got them right yet. The part of his argument which I believe to be most valid falls into two areas which, even though I find my own sympathies lie elsewhere, serve to highlight the danger areas for the de-massifiers

These two danger points will be addressed in Part Four when we look at implementation ideas for the future. They are:

Danger Point 1 – Professor Jacques suggests, rather like my own view of communism, that non-hierarchies defy human nature. As individuals, we want a pecking order and we want a ladder to climb. He argues that people feel more comfortable and work better in this environment.

Danger point 2 – Professor Jacques holds severe doubts about the way groups, as distinct from individuals, can be held accountable.

In an article published in the *Harvard Business Review* in 1990 under the title 'In Praise of Hierarchy', Jacques writes: 'It [hierarchy] is the only form of organisation that can enable a company to employ large numbers of people and yet preserve unambiguous accountability for the work they do.' He concludes the article with 'hierarchy is the best structure for getting work done in big organisations'. A flaw in this argument may lie in the thought that most users of the fragmentation concept are creating a network of small organisations out of the large one. In my own view, if there is evidence that hierarchies work well in your business, it may be better to break up the business into smaller units and create small hierarchies than to suffer the imperfections and burdens of a large one.

The concept of work groups or teams, a system about which Professor Jacques is also concerned, is often talked about as new and innovative. The notion is, it is said, that a leader supported by multiplexed disciplined colleagues of equal or similar status is an unproven commodity, yet, to me, it sounds for all the world like the perfect description of a board of directors, a group which, I think, can claim a fairly well-proven case.

The prime resource of tomorrow's marketer

Whichever or whatever structure you choose, the single most important resource for the future is the marketing database (as distinct from database marketing). The ability to access information (or, indeed, the ability to find the data to process and turn into information) will become the issue around which all other issues revolve in the future. Information is, in this context, power, in that it is the future commodity of marketing. As both sides fragment, communications and logistical problems increase, although bureaucracy and waste decrease. So no great step can be taken towards total quality marketing without the ability to move and process information around the network; or indeed, to provide the built-in monitor, the finger on the pulse, the control systems. Total quality marketing focuses on improved human interaction. It takes time. It feeds on information. Quality improves not only the nature of transactions and communications but also the quantity of them. The database will prove to be the key to the effectiveness of your personal and corporate marketing effort.

In Chapter 11, we discovered that our new workplaces are likely to be quite different. Marketing as a function has as much reason to fragment as the organisations it takes to market. The points covered were:

- Middle management now performs a large data-processing function, much of which can be handled automatically or differently in the future.

- Many firms are finding that redeploying such skilled and literate people at the Customer end of the business makes better use of them and increases Customer satisfaction.

- To be most effective, marketers may need to consider fragments of fragments, niche marketing for niche markets.

- In analysing and quantifying the problem – THINK CUSTOMER. Look at yourself from the Customer's perception and appraise what real benefits will be lost when the structure breaks up.

- The aim of such fragmentation (as it refers to total quality marketing) is that it enables marketers to involve themselves in, and in some cases lead, the building and maintenance of Customer relationships. Marketing is therefore not a corporate resource; it is an integral part of the product or service.

- If you believe hierarchies work well and you are in a big corporation, an alternative to group or teamwork could be to restructure into smaller hierarchies.

- The two significant risk areas for group work are that it could be less than satisfactory in relation to human nature's historically preferred method – the hierarchy – and that it is less successful in matters of accountability.

- A major and prerequisite central resource of total quality marketing is the marketing database.

- Total quality marketing improves both the nature and number of Customer transactions and communications.

12

Looking Back into the Future

For business the future gets harder. For marketing, it gets harder still. There is such a long way to go, so much lost time to recoup, such an appalling lack of quality standards to correct, so much happening all around us, so much to learn anew.

We've already looked at some of the major factors; but there exist many others, of course, not the least of which are the three commodities required to take total quality marketing into your organisation. These are money, time and courage.

Pressure on the margin

As we progress through the 1990s and the quality aspects start to recover, the added-value perceptions that we give the Customer will decrease price sensitivity. In a sense the only people locked into a price-sensitive situation should be those stupid enough to get themselves into it in the first place, or those equally stupid not to have taken the opportunity to move out of it. The slackening of pressure on price will be gratefully received because elsewhere the margin will be at severe stretch. Consider the list of items queuing up for a greater share:

- Product development: can you afford not to keep up the pace as product life cycles get shorter?

- The increasing demands of the Customer: quality and design cost money; can you recover all of it?

- The decreasing cost-effectiveness of the media: you'll need a bigger budget to have the same effect.

- Internationalisation: going international or global is an expensive business before it yields rewards – even if you're only looking for partners.

- Customer service and Customer care: both of these aspects of total quality marketing cost more money. The good news is that some things can self-liquidate and, therefore, at least spread the budget a little.

- The need to build corporate image and positioning: some of this work can be carried out along with advertising, but the rest needs funding.

- Building and running the marketing database; any database is only as useful as it is accurate and up-to-date.

- Quality dedication means picking the best staff and then training them: training levels, if you have a good standard now, will increase by 50 per cent; if less than good, your new budget will need to double or treble. If you're British you have another problem, details following.

So you see the margin will come under stress. How much of this is passed on and how much must be financed by improvement elsewhere is for you, your competitors and your market to establish.

While considering the pressures that will apply to margins in the future, I think it is possible that the 'Europisation' of companies (or even globalisation) might cause further stress. I have strong views about where retailers should exercise their strength – and particularly where they must show greater care. I am most concerned about so much pressure being applied that their manufacturers or suppliers are squeezed to a point where they can no longer control their margins and therefore, in effect, no longer run their own businesses. One very real threat to margins could emerge from the arrival of Euro-super-group retailers.

There is a great deal of activity – acquisitions, mergers and equity exchanges – taking place at the moment. Should this lead to a level of Europe-wide central buying in which the needs of all members of the alliance or partnership are consolidated to increase the buying power, then the results will, I suspect, be quite negative for the consumer in the long run. Furthermore, while such centralised mass negotiations may make sense from the retailer's position, they are entirely against the interests of both the Customer and the original manufacturer. Such arrangements may succeed for a while with basic commodities but are generally contrary to the predicted direction for Customer requirements.

The battle with time

Quality takes time to implement. It has to become woven into the fabric of the company; so, for that matter, does putting the Customer first. Many businesses seem not to have been created for their Customers. They exist to produce or manufacture or process; they have to buy, to administer, to look after their staff. They have to pay suppliers and bill their Customers. And, oh yes! They have to sell. To such organisations, making every major decision a 'Customer first' decision is very difficult. And even when the decision is made, implementing it is also arduous.

The time it takes to set total quality marketing in place will depend not just on the size of your company, but also on the number of people and locations involved, and the amount of restructuring and reorganisation that has to be done. This is a programme that will probably take quite a while – a year at least, maybe two or three more. The key question is how much of a march you can steal over your competitors by getting started quickly.

And a whole heap of courage

Total quality marketing also needs courage. And, I would add, perseverance. For the first two or even three years, little benefit may be gained, while probably most of the set-up costs will be incurred.

We shall look later at the fascinating case history of Rank Xerox. After three years' investment in quality it reported no visible improvement. In the fourth year real gains began to be seen and by the fifth year, a veritable fireworks display of benefits: profits up 40 per cent, return on assets effectively trebled, unit costs of components down by 30 per cent and, most important of all, Customer satisfaction up 35 per cent. Rich rewards!

However, this all goes to prove that old habits die hard – especially bad ones.

The unique problems of the UK

As the world of business and commerce moves towards quality, not just in marketing, but throughout its disciplines, the UK, sadly, will find itself with a severe handicap, for the British appreciation of quality standards is by far the lowest of the major European industrials, and is no better measured on a world scale.

It is not for this book to lay blame; indeed, in a generous moment you could blame society in general.

The problem starts with the consumer; UK mass markets are the least discerning in the world. In business the belief in quality as a necessity hardly exists; it seems to be viewed almost as a luxury and a practice for those who want to be at the very top of the tree – a place where many think the whole thing is just too much trouble.

The UK has an awful lot of middle; there's enough pride left to want to stay off the bottom, but absolutely no desire to be at the top. The 'middle's OK' attitude becomes most obvious when we come under threat. Give the Brits a war to fight or the most difficult recession in history to overcome – no problem! Out comes the latest version of the 'I'm backing Britain' campaign, and the foot hits the floor. But no sooner has the corner been turned, than we want to put up our feet, have a cup of tea and get back to the telly. When you're up against American drive, French creativity, German quality and Japanese everything, the UK has to realise that competing is not something which can be attended to in fits and starts.

Quality starts at birth and at home

The fact is that the UK education system is delivering lower-quality young people to industry and commerce than it needs. UK standards are dropping when our competitors' are rising (see Fig. 12.1) Thus, UK industry has to train its young intake to get them up to speed before they can be used. This decline has been taking place for a decade or more and, whatever the colour of the governments of the future, it will take at least a decade to correct.

The correction, however, does not lie simply within UK schools. Quality is a way of life, and the value standards generally in the UK no longer demand sufficient quality. This problem, I believe, dates back to the 1960s.

I would love to have to confess that I am some arrogant, pompous cantankerous old rat, and that my view is the result of being sworn at by some hooligan. Sorry, it's not that! Mine are the views of someone who travels the world as a trainer and consultant, and who sees the literate, articulate, educated, enthusiastic,

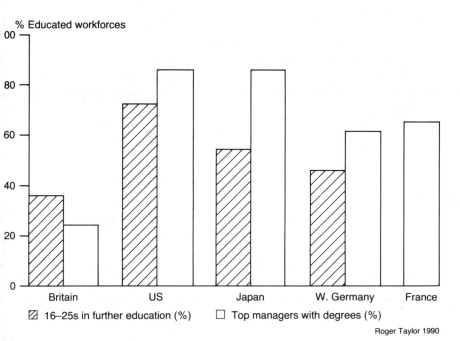

% Educated workforces

Source: *Business Magazine*

Figure 12.1: Education at work – where the UK stands against its competitors in relation to managers with degrees and young people in further education.

and most often multilingual youngsters that other countries enjoy.

I wish there was an answer to this dilemma. The only one I can suggest is to be ruthless in your recruitment, generous in your training, fastidious in your monitoring of standards, and as demanding as possible in all matters of quality.

I should add that this predicament causes me pain. I'm British and proud of it, as the saying goes. Nothing would give me greater pleasure than to heap praise on British young people, and junior or trainee workers, executives and managers; but it's just not possible. I further realise that not everyone is at fault and that there are many shining examples of well-brought-up, well-educated, and socially and culturally admirable young men and women; but, sadly, they exist in nothing like the numbers the UK needs to hold top positions in global industries and commerce by the turn of the century.

Quality suffers no dropouts

The quality of the young is important because total quality marketing is a practice for businesses of every size, from one-man bands to vast multinationals. It is a culture, a philosophy, and a creed as well as a strategy and a system. It is also by far the most competitive action you can take. However, it is not a movement of which you can opt out. 'Quality is not for me' will be an epitaph, not a decision.

Quality turns back the clock

Before there were so many of us, businesses delivered quality as a norm. Shopping used to be a pleasure; recognition an everyday occurrence; customised service the way it was; courtesy and value part of the deal. And that is where we have to get back to. This is a numbers problem. If we all had fewer Customers, we could devote more time to them, think more about them and dedicate more of our resources to their problems. It is therefore a conundrum which many of us will solve through computers and technology, the database being a prime example. The other method is actually to arrange fewer Customers; to break your marketing thrust down into smaller units which will market to smaller groups of Customers.

At one time I found myself referring to the past, the way things used to be, how our parents and grandparents experienced things, so often that I began to be very self-conscious about it. I sounded more like an ageing historian than someone fascinated by the way business is changing for the future.

Yet it's not coincidence. In the past it was better in quality and service terms, and it will improve again. All we have to do is recognise the gravity of the problem, appreciate the speed with which we must get started and understand the lengths to which we must go to get back to the future of total quality marketing.

This chapter draws to a close Part Two of *Total Quality Marketing*, in which we have reviewed some of the key issues that will affect marketing through the 1990s and into the next century. Next we will look at the steps we must take to prepare for the age of satisfaction marketing. But first, our chapter review:

● Great pressure will build up on prices and margins. The need to be competitive must be balanced against the desire to maintain product development; to meet the demands of the Customer; to cope with decreasing media effectiveness; to go international; to meet the costs of increased Customer-care programmes; to increase the budget for corporate image and positioning; to build and maintain a database; and to spend more on recruitment and training.

● Total quality marketing is a process which requires time, perseverance and persistence to yield its rewards.

● A great deal of courage is required by the board and senior managers since the payback for total quality marketing is slow, but when it comes, rich and long-term.

● The UK has a severe quality handicap which will be industry's problem to sort out in the short term. In the long term it can only be hoped that quality will become a way of life in more ways than one.

● You can't duck the quality race. It's merely a question of when you get started.

● To put quality into marketing will, for many, be a restoration process. We're headed back to the future as fast as we can!

Part Three: In Preparation

13

Trends

Part Two of this book identified many of the changes you will see taking place in marketing during the following years, discussed some of the problems you will face, and looked at some positive ideas which might hold the key to the ways you react and respond to threats and opportunities; and we saw how those will abound in the agitated yet challenging and stimulating times in front of us.

By the end we had painted a picture of an inevitable outcome – business will get harder, but marketing will get harder still. Is this the kind of gloomy scaremongering you buy books for? Certainly, whether we like to face it or not, it doesn't get any easier out there in the future; therefore, I would like to look now at some of the preparations we can make. At least, if it's going to rain, we can get our waterproofs on!

This next section is to help move us into preparation mode, and it contains plenty more ideas; but, particularly, they are ideas that identify the major issues to think about and what you can do about them. All of which should help you to review your own practices and adjust them to the ways that will maximise your success in the new marketing environment.

Some of the issues we'll consider are quite mundane, pragmatic ideas; others are conceptual or philosophical; but all of them are critical to marketing effectiveness. We will consider new criteria for choosing what is currently called an advertising agency: we will look at how many agencies a big-budget marketer should have – and, where it's more than one, how the work should be divided among them. We'll endeavour to form a closer, more detailed understanding of the ways that selling and marketing will change, and take a look at the fundamental processes of buying and selling; and, finally, in Part Three, we will examine new concepts as granular marketing is explained.

This all leads into Part Four, where methods are demonstrated by which you will most successfully implement the kinds of changes that the future needs from you.

Connecting the dots

One of my most frequently used slides for the beginning of training sessions is taken from a cartoon strip. A prisoner lies festering in a dark, damp medieval dungeon. Peering through the bars of the tiny hole in his cell door, he calls out to his jailer. With obvious pride he explains that he has just finished a book he has been working on and proffers it to the jailer. The next two frames show the prisoner waiting expectantly for the praise and congratulations he is sure will issue forth – the jailer, on the other hand, is clearly puzzled, unable to make any sense of it. He turns to the prisoner, who seeing his puzzlement, explains, 'You've got to connect the dots!'

In a sense, before we move on to the next layer of information, that's what I would like to do now; otherwise, we run the danger of, as the saying goes, simply being confused – but at a much higher level.

The rise and rise of the Customer

Surely, it is the return of the Customer as the raison d'être of marketing which is behind the need for total quality marketing. That's not to say that Customers place quality first in all their purchasing; of course not. They are often looking for a value balance, which may include many factors. However, the new breed of marketers are convinced that, when you look at today's marketing environment, capturing the Customer's heart, trust and loyalty is a highly potent cocktail which has fascinatingly attractive after effects. It certainly is, for example, extraordinarily strong at locking out competitiors. In an age when 'We'll beat any price in town', and 'Free Credit' signs have become commonplace in the High Street, marketing seems to have reached a stage where duelling competitiors, having run out of ammunition and broken their swords, are now reduced to rolling round in the mud slugging it out until one of them finally drops. Is that marketing? I think not. It's the result of a business that has worshipped quantity at any price, and done so for so long, that every last drop of quality-based thinking has been wrung out of it to the point that it is absolutely quality-parched.

Take a look at the state that this transaction-marketing, 'close that sale' mentality has left as its inheritance; there you can see the roots of so many of the problems we have given ourselves.

Develop a quality lock

So this is the start of our new cultivation process, a barren desert. No better place to start! And in this desert there is beginning to blow a strong wind of change. It is blowing now and it is the wind of quality. It carries the message that the bond created with the Customer is far greater than the sum of the transactions.

For those who change direction first, it holds the most difficult task, but a commensurate reward. Those who establish the strongest, most enduring relationships now will be those who hold the high ground. It is extremely difficult for a competitor to wrestle away a Customer who enjoys a broad-based, satisfying relationship with you. Those who inherit the task of attacking competitors who have developed a quality lock on their market will have a daunting task ahead of them. It will cost them dear in time, effort, resources and cash.

However, let us also remember at this time, the principle of marketing as a three-way process; it should encompass, not only your market but also your people and your suppliers too. This will add longevity, loyalty and endurance in these areas, thus affording safety and stability to its practitioners.

Trends to turmoil

So why is all this necessary? Is the argument in favour of a return to quality purely a flimsy emotional cry ... or are there really things happening out there that point to it unequivocally as the way forward.

Certainly, if you look at the way things were headed as we left the 1980s, you could be forgiven for becoming quite pessimistic or depressed. Throughout the world we witnessed many trends which suggested that the rewards of marketing, as distinct from the rewards of selling (as I differentiated them in Chapters 7 and 8), would make a change of direction necessary. The notions of a chaotic, unpredictable business environment are well forecast, and much advice is being issued. Indeed, for many, this was the starting point for the quality rationale. It remains a mystery why so very, very few extended that to include their marketing. None the less, the beginning of the 1990s saw the global ranks of marketers in the developed world facing an array of problems to handle.

Think about it. While the world saw increasing seesaw swings in its economic fortunes, many marketers found themselves with the twin conundrum of mature markets and parallel products. Those same markets were becoming more and more fragmented and diverse while the media were offering less and less effectiveness. In terms of distribution, again right across the world we saw a startling level of change developing in their patterns, a level of change, which, in turn provoked power shifts which were often as rapid as they were short-lived and ill-conceived. Many quite large and previously soundly based businesses were acquired by rapid growth corporations which found themselves overextended and caught on the hop by violent interest-rate fluctuations. Suddenly, even some of the blue chip names became less solid and dependable. This unsatisfactory state soon led to a consequent nervousness in the tents of the moneylenders. And rightly so. They had lent too much too easily for too long. Now, with their minds refocused on the financial picture and on belt-tightening, companies found themselves drawing in and cutting back, just as the wholly materialistic and greedy business of transaction-based selling backfired and led them into markets which had forced Customer expectation to rise, while often also becoming more price sensitive.

The timing could not have been worse. Competition both domestic and foreign was mounting while, simultaneously, their weapons were proving less effective; marketing effectiveness was declining, while the pressure was pouring on, with constant changes in technology, costly in themselves, but more difficult still when you saw how those same technologies shortened the life cycles of products and services. A competitive advantage got more difficult to gain and more expensive to establish, and it lasted for shorter and shorter periods.

I rest half my case! The half that says circumstances, whether accidental or created by marketers themselves, have led us to a point where the only logical solution in all this turbulence is to create calm and stability: to bring back practices that breed long-term criteria and professionalism.

If that wasn't enough evidence to support total quality marketing, based as it is around the creation and maintenance of relationships, not transactions, there is another convincing case which requires simply that one read the signs and consider what to do next. Again total quality marketing is the only logical answer. See if you agree.

Let's return to those issues raised in Chapter 8 on pages 80–1 when we discovered Professor Louis Stern's array of corporate, product marketing and marketing mix strategies (Tables 8.1, 8.2 and 8.3).

Table 13.1: The synergy of strategies

Line no.	1990 Strategy	Correlations
1. Product/market strategies		
1.1	Niche & customised marketing and product positioning	1: 2 3 4 5 6 7 2: 1 2 3 4 5 6 3: 1 2 3 4 5 6
1.2	Customer/competitor/channel orientation	1: 1 3 4 5 6 7 2: 1 2 3 4 5 6 3: 1 2 3 4 5 6
1.3	Product line rationalisation	1: 1 2 4 5 7 2: 1 2 3 4 5 6 3: 1 2 4 5
1.4	Strategic mission for each product	1: 1 2 3 4 7 2: 1 2 3 4 5 6 3: 1 2 4 5
1.5	Selective market coverage	1: 1 2 3 4 7 2: 4 5 6 3: 2 4
1.6	Global marketing	1: 1 2 3 4 5 6 2: 1 2 4 3: 1 2 3 4 5
1.7	Local marketing	1: 1 2 3 4 5 6 2: 1 2 4 5 6 3: 1 2 3 4 5 6
2. Marketing mix strategies		
2.1	Decision support system research	1: 1 2 3 4 6 7 2: 2 3 4 5 3: 1 2 3 4 5
2.2	Competing on quality, design and services	1: 1 2 3 4 6 7 2: 1 3 4 5 6 3: 1 2 3 4 5 6
2.3	Pricing based on Customer perceived value	1: 1 2 3 4 2: 1 2 4 3: 2
2.4	Suppliers/distributors as partners	1: 1 2 3 4 5 6 7 2: 1 2 3 5 6 3: 1 2 3 4 5 6

Table 13.1 continued

Line no.	1990 Strategy	Correlations
2.5	Multiplexed salesforces	1: 2 3 4 5 7
		2: 1 2 4 6
		3: 2 4 5 6
2.6	Targeted and co-ordinated communications	
		1: 1 2 3 4 5 7
		2: 2 4 5
		3: 2 6
3. Corporate strategies		
3.1	Synergistic diversification	1: 1 2 3 4 6 7
		2: 1 2 4
		3: 2 3 4 5 6
3.2	Implementation excellence	1: 1 2 3 4 5 6 7
		2: 1 2 3 4 5 6
		3: 1 3 4 5 6
3.3	Economies of scope	1: 1 2 6 7
		2: 1 2 4
		3: 1 2 4 5 6
3.4	Governance structures	1: 1 2 3 4 5 6 7
		2: 1 2 4
		3: 1 2 3 5 6
3.5	Strategic alliances	1: 1 2 3 4 6 7
		2: 1 2 4 5
		3: 1 2 3 4 6
3.6	Co-ordinated business functions	
		1: 1 2 7
		2: 2 4 5 6
		3: 1 2 3 4 5

This table identifies the quite staggering synergy between the strategies when relationship building and total quality marketing are the objective. To use the table: each of the strategies listed has a strategy-type prefix and a line-number suffix. To identify the strategies of importance when considering the quality issues, the corresponding numbers are given in the right-hand column headed Correlations. Remarkably, of the potential 57 lines, 37 have more than 5 correlating strategies. This illustrates the strength and cohesion of the force behind quality concepts in marketing for the future.

Look back and consider how many of those from the 1990s column point in the same direction. With only two or three exceptions which, as it were, rest in a neutral position, the remainder stand together pointing clearly towards the ways of relationship-centred activities. For example, take niche and customised marketing and product positioning; Customer, competitor, channel orientation; strategic mission for each product; and product line rationalisation; the multiplex salesforce; targeted and co-ordinated communications; pricing based on Customer-perceived values; suppliers and distributors as friends; governance structures; strategic alliances; and synergistic diversification. Each one of those and others, if they don't actually suggest or support relationship marketing values and ideas, will prosper and flourish best in such an environment.

That's the other half of the case. Once you have understood the significance and force of its direction, its inevitability is clear. To add weight to all of this, consider the table opposite which shows again the full list from Chapter 8, this time with the addition of a key which enables you to identify which and how the factors correlate. It's a formidable network of synergy, serving to add one final compelling force to my arguments.

If you draw the conclusion that there is no time to be wasted in adopting total quality marketing, then we would be in accord. Let's move on to look at some of the ways you can start putting the quality back into marketing. Before we do, here is the summary of this chapter:

- The evidence to support the adoption of quality techniques in marketing is quite overwhelming.

- As the 1980s ended, the trends in business environment consisted of two predominant types: the first was the result of marketing's obsession with quantity for three decades or more; the second, more circumstantial but totally endorsing of the new quality directions.

- Of the major informed academic projections, once the picture has been pieced together, these, too, suggest the same path. Quality must return to provide the deeper, longer-lasting relationships which will satisfy the Customer's needs and provide the stability, sales and profitability which is required to finance them.

14

The New Wave Client for the New Wave Agency

Here it comes again! Another idea through which we're going back to the future. In the 1950s and early 1960s many advertising agencies claimed to be 'one-stop shops'. They wanted to be all things to all people; they failed, but tried quite hard. They laid claim to corporate image; to general brochure and leaflet work; and to all sales promotion activities, branding and packaging, and direct mail. You name it, they did it. Or said they did. They had merchandising departments and public-relations departments, and some even had marketing departments – marketing in that context proving to be a euphemism for 'below-the-line'. Yet what they were good at was advertising. Above-the-line they were all-powerful; below-the-line, all-greedy.

The expression 'jack of all trades, master of none' was never more appropriate. The skills they applied below-the-line were often ill-conceived, ill-planned and ill-informed. Watching the appalling mistakes and waste, the business quickly spawned a highly skilled, efficient and competitive host of marketing service suppliers who have been there ever since; some of them pulled together a set of discrete disciplines to which they could apply discrete skills. Direct marketing agencies are a perfect example. In the 1960s, so frustrated by the mess the big agencies were making of, particularly, the strategy and creativity of their discipline, many mailing houses, specialist printers, house-to-house distributors and their counterparts set up their own competitive sources. They quickly improved the results Clients were getting and, since they often sold to Clients directly, effectively positioned themselves in competition with the agencies and became rivals for the budgets.

Apart from improving the strategic use of marketing services and increasing the cost-effectiveness which resulted, little else positive was achieved. Indeed, a holy war started. The above-the-line on one side – the establishment – well backed and financed by the City in London and Wall Street in the US; arrogant, in control, the natural home of 90 per cent of the budget. On the other side – the wrong side of the tracks – was the unshaven vocal and rebellious rabble that was below-the-line. Even the phrase itself gives away the 'bad smell under the nose' way with which classical advertising people mouthed this distasteful description. And just to make absolutely sure the below-the-liners knew their place, the agencies asked them to use the tradesman's entrance and deal with the print buyers and media buyers.

Ultimately, it was the Client who was to make a decision, and in so doing, start to resolve the issue. Ironically, it leads us back to the 1950s.

Divided we stand, divided we fall

The marketing services specialists and their allies were not to be so easily discouraged. They had ambition, they had valuable and demonstrably cost-efficient skills, and they had the conviction of the underdog, with all the energy, enthusiasm and cunning that being shown the tradesman's entrance was to engender. Yes, perhaps I should add resentment. Through the 1970s, the below-the-line voices got louder as their skills became more polished and accomplished. Gradually they started to squeeze the agencies by their jugulars; in other words – their budget share.

It was a two-faced, hypocritical holy war. On the surface both sides claimed friendship and co-operation; underneath they spat venom at each other. The below-the-line specialists were creatively incompetent; they undermined brand values, and were often strategic vandals – no better than greedy guerrillas. Those above-the-line were arrogant, overpriced, overrated and obsessed with television. As in all good holy wars – or rather bad ones – both sides were right; both sides were wrong.

So by the late 1970s, marketers were faced with a choice of classical ad agencies for their account – which was essentially their mass-media spend, together with their choice from a wide range of specialist suppliers. There were effective, highly skilled sources for corporate design, packaging, public relations, sales promotion, sponsorship and events, and, of course, the major growth area – and some would argue (foolishly in my view), the contender for the throne – direct marketing.

Strangely, I don't think the war will ever be decisively won or lost. Individual Clients may choose one way or the other for a time, but broadly, across the business, another resolution will occur. The best will be plucked from both or all sides.

Clients must take the initiative

The fact is that, strategically at least, the Client was the loser – neither the above-the-line nor the below-the-line side was providing unbiased strategic advice. They were both providing advice which was almost always biased (not unnaturally!) and almost always tactical. Inevitably, the major criterion for any proposition placed before the Client was to secure the spending and thereby the welfare of the proposer. Which agency in their right mind would advise a Client to reduce his budget by 50 per cent and hand it out to the specialist; which specialist was going to tell the Client that he was overspending on sales promotion, was a fraction low on direct marketing, should hold it where it was on PR, and up his radio and national dailies? Thus, the Clients made the decisions, some better than others, naturally.

Where are we now? – where should we go?

The position is now very confused. Some agencies have 'acquired' specialists. Of those, some have merged them in; others keep them as service companies within the group; still others just take an interest and let them operate autonomously. PR and design have managed, by and large, to remain distinct disciplines, whereas direct marketing and sales promotion seem to be confused by many companies, one as a function or technique of the other. There is some overlap, of course, but really the confusion has little logic, other than that they are both deeply rooted in the business of quantity-based selling; but then isn't all marketing at the moment?

To make total quality marketing happen, it is necessary to return to the one-stop-shop concept, with one less than subtle difference. Instead of the agencies merely wanting to do it all, they genuinely have to be able to deliver. In order to deliver, they will need to acquire or merge with – and *fully integrate* – the specialists. This means the disciplines may have 'centres of excellence' so to speak, within the agency, but there must be competent planning, creative and implementation skills available to the Client on a day-to-day basis. Thus, agencies will need creative, media and account-handling personnel who are trained and skilled on a much broader, more general basis. Specialist service suppliers will need to have the vision and confidence to abandon their single skill specialisation and take their rightful place in the establishment. Clients may

thus – as they need to reduce the size of their marketing department anyway – let go of the buying and administrative roles they
have developed to deal with all the marketing services suppliers;
then they can consolidate and pull back to the functions of control.
Clients must become judges again, not referees. Thus, we shall see
the gradual transformation within the establishment block, from
advertising agency to integrated marketing agency.

This now poses two further questions: where should the strategic
thinking take place; and how will big accounts be divided up, if
indeed, they should?

Where will the thinking be done?

Those agencies who can demonstrate a truly integrated service, no
doubt will deserve an opportunity to be involved in the short-,
medium- and long-term strategy. Indeed, I suspect that one of the
spin-offs of the new wave Client is that he, like the rest of the world,
will become aware of the benefit of longer-term relationships; thus,
most Clients will place more value on the teamwork and spirit that
develops on both sides when practising TQM methods. However, I
remain uncertain that the agency – integrated or not – is the best
place, from the Client's point of view, for planning. I believe the
optimum place for such planning will be among a new breed of
'super consultants' and 'strategic business planners' whom we are
already beginning to see develop – often specialising, as they will
probably have to continue to do, in certain fields. Perhaps the best-
known example of them is James Martin, the multimillionaire
strategic consultant, who has made a worldwide consultancy and
training business in the technology and computer field.

My preference for the independent planning and strategic
counsel is not founded on the basis that agencies are unable to
prepare strategic plans, nor that they are incapable of the quality
levels required. I am sure they will acquire the necessary people
and, in time, retrain their staff accordingly. My concern is that I
remain sceptical that those who profit from the way the money is
spent are the best people to decide how it should be spent. As I
have demonstrated, agencies have already proven that this is an
irresistible temptation for them. I think this represents a strong case
for a separate strategic-planning function, and I am sure there will
be a mushrooming of such consultancies and plenty of work for
them. My experience has been that the only major snag in using

separate planners, with the agency implementing the plans later, is that of accountability for successes and failures. Which is responsible, the plan or its implementation methods, tactics and ideas? The best advice I can give is to understand that using an independent strategist does not preclude agency involvement. I would encourage the presence of a group from the agency in the planning sessions, thus developing tacit acceptance of the plans, increased consideration of the implementation issues and, if no more tangible link, at least a spirit of mutual commitment to, and accountability for, the plans generated.

And how will Clients decide who gets what?

There are some ideas now in use which can be improved upon as you move into total quality marketing. Let's take a typical arrangement at the moment. Suppose you're a company with four brands or product groups. Often each of these will have the freedom to choose its own agency; similarly, each of those same groups will appoint or, less formally, buy regularly from its own choice of secondary specialist agency, backed up or supported by a whole host of PR, direct marketing, sales promotion, research, packaging and design specialists.

In organisational terms, Clients seem to have developed the people and the systems to deal with this, and when one considers the brand or product group issues, it often works well. However, as we move into the 'brand behind the brand', and the need becomes greater for a uniform corporate voice, such processes will break down or underperform. It makes no sense to have a corporate message diffused, distorted or interpreted countless different ways. It confuses the market and works badly for the company.

A simple idea solves a complex problem

Shouting at the market in 10, 15 or 20 different voices could become just one more dimension in the build-up to the communications traffic jam. There is a simple answer.

I have always taken the view that there are only three kinds of Customer: the existing Customer, the prospective Customer, and the lapsed or past Customer. It is generally accepted and agreed that in terms of effectiveness from the marketing unit of currency, the highest return will come from existing Customers (a performance difference typically of some 500 to 1500 per cent) and the lowest return from prospects. However, the second-highest return comes from the Customer so many people seem to overlook – or write off – the lapsed or past Customer.

Examining this, I have concluded that if – and only if – you are able to work with an integrated agency, the best way to divide the workload is by appointing the agency – across the product groups or brands – making them guardians of the relationship.

Casting your mind back to the thoughts expressed concerning the communications traffic jam, you can well understand that, if messages are confused before they leave and confused again as they leave, the result is going to be mayhem from the Customer's point of view. So, rather than have our communications disturbed and distorted, we need to find ways to improve their integrity.

There is no doubt that integration or fusion of the advertising, sales and Customer service messages is one very positive step forward. Indeed, we are already seeing some steps towards the provision of such integrated services by some of the more forward-looking groups and networks.

It must be realised that integrated communications, as a fundamental factor in the overall process of total communications management, are pre-requisite to the concept of relationship marketing. However, the most common stumbling block I have seen is that the long-term objectives of relationship marketing, like so many quality issues, require agreement, acceptance and commitment at the very highest level. At the moment, awareness of the re-blossoming importance of such issues is rarely recognised among the board; therefore, marketing directors, however committed they may be personally, can have great difficulty in carrying their colleagues along with them. Often only one, or possibly two, of the board will truly appreciate what is at stake. It is no surprise therefore that the lead is being taken by those companies who already have either a marketer at the top or a healthily pro-marketing environment on the board. Good vision is certainly a useful lubricant to the right decisions here.

By the end of the 1990s the influences which we have already discussed will push two options to the front. There is no doubt that the first of these is actually a compromise which will enable a quite workable face-lift to be carried out.

Option one: more people

In order to deliver the new relationship-style of Customer service – and therefore the intensity of staffing required to provide the optimum server/Customer ratio, marketers will have to restructure their front end (the face they display to their Customers). Control and monitoring of this extended, as it were, broadside exposure of their front line would be handled on a database; Customer communications of whatever type will be focused via, or in support of, the individual Customer servicer or Customer-services team, but always through or acknowledged by, a database.

This will lead to an increase in teams, in many ways structured in the style familiar to marketers, similar to those found inside advertising agencies: a triangular-shaped team with three or four levels. However, I described this as cosmetic and a compromise. And it is so. For, on a short-term basis, it will enable the Customer to feel as if he were getting more service. What is actually happening is that the Customer is getting more attention. This is not in itself a problem, but it is still far short of what is needed for a truly effective relationship to develop. For, such service teams are usually long on bonhomie and rhetoric but short on the authority and decision-making capability that is needed.

So why is this a compromise? Why is it less likely to succeed? Consider this scenario. In comes a wealth of new communications technology. This is irresistible to people involved in Customer service. And, understandably; after all, a lot of the time the pressure to accept or adopt new hi-tech communications methods or media comes from the markets or Customers they serve.

Next let's fuel this with the certain knowledge that the easiest way to show a quick, or cosmetic, increase in Customer care or service is to communicate more, stay in touch, keep the Customer informed. This means, of course, that in order to make the necessary impression on Customers, more people in more departments will want to communicate more ways through more media. And if you're dealing with an organisation, more people will receive these communications across correspondingly more departments. Think of the recipe this becomes for confusion and irritation. Simply stir in the media and technology explosions which we see happening in parallel and bake well. Soon you'll have a perfect disaster in the making. All covered in that confection of the future – the communications traffic jam!

Option two: more sense

Option one is only for those who want an interim measure before option two or those who are content with the cosmetic improvement. Option two is for those who want the real thing; but it does mean you must seek out suppliers who offer you integrated marketing services, and then appoint them as guardians of one of the three basic relationships.

Reverting to my 'three kinds of Customer', you will see that in your forward marketing thrust, you are basically cultivating three corresponding categories of relationship, as illustrated in the table below:

Table 14.1: Relationship styles and objectives

Category	Style	Objective
Prospects	Warming	Acquisition
Customers	Satisfying	Growth
Lapsed/past Customers	Restoring	Reconciliation

To maintain the integrity of corporate voices, the responsibility for communications should be divided within these relationship objectives. Thus, one agency might be appointed guardian of existing Customers; this agency will have demonstrated its ability to create powerful advertising and sales messages which respect Customers, understand their needs, and speak with one corporate voice. As with the other two categories, this cuts across all brands, products or services. Only where there is no 'cross-talk' or cross-selling opportunity with brands would division of guardianship by brand be recommended.

This clearly suggests that the formal division between the disciplines (advertising, sales promotion, direct marketing, PR, etc), running as they do in tightly defined alleys, must dissolve or at least assume far less priority. The overall basket of media, and the uses to which those media are put, will fall along with the whole gamut of Customer service activities into a total communications management environment. There, with the marketing database as its core resource, the individual relationship with the Customer will take its rightful place as the driving force. This should provide a perfect culture for optimum Customer service levels and qualities. In those companies where marketing and sales remain uneasy bedfellows, such new thinking will be difficult to accept since they must clearly come together as one redefined effort.

So, the new picture will include fused sales and marketing teams also dividing their efforts into the three steps of acquisition, growth and reconciliation.

Agencies must cease to divide themselves according to the worn-out departmental thinking of the 1960s, 1970s and 1980s. What most affects their achievement for Clients is the weighting of the message and media dependent upon which of the three objectives and relationships they have been given custody.

This is a necessary return to some of the ways of the past. However, this time it is imperative that the ability be there to deliver the specialist skills required across the board by today's marketer. This change will cause the development of very different agencies. With the added dimension of the Customer relationship as a specific, briefed criterion of effectiveness, it should breed a rather more professional, less cynical and less exploitative type of organisation. In the prospecting area, I suspect that sales-promotional techniques will continue to prevail, feeding on the human weaknesses which have been their diet for so long. Thus, this particular style of agency may be the nearest to the current style.

Of course, many agencies will claim to be the master of all three styles; indeed, they may well prove this capabilty. However, my suspicion is that the styles – warming, satisfying and restoring – may become, as time passes and the specialisations build expertise, really very different in practice.

So the heydays of many of the distinct disciplines may be over. Will we see the death of direct marketing, the demise of PR, or the end of sales promotion? I don't think so! There will, of course, be many special cases, or smaller Clients who will continue to use the resources of marketing services as we know them now. But in ten years' time the serious spenders will have gone back to the 1950s and once again appointed their agencies to do it all. These agencies are being born right now. They are the result of new ideas, new thinking, new Customer needs and desires, new technology and a new environment.

From which stable will the lead to integrated marketing come?

There is a slow but sure appreciation of the benefits of integrated marketing in the advertising and marketing worlds. One or two international, direct-marketing groups are claiming to have invented it – which is patent nonsense. However, I suspect that the front position will be taken from somewhere in Martin Sorrell's WPP Group.

Some unkind things have been said of Sorrell – notably that he is a better accountant than an advertising man. If this is so, I suspect he is a very skilled accountant. It is clear from some of the activities within his group, together with his own finely-tuned vision, that he has the integrated direction in mind. Although he has quite strong views about 'one-stop shops' (he suggests there is an implication in them of diminished capabilities), he has aimed to provide all the services within the group. While this will not work satisfactorily for long – indeed, I have discussed the shortfall with a disappointed WPP Group Client – it is clear that the skills and resources and, most importantly, the understanding and practice of integrated marketing techniques will be ready to make that final jump when Sorrell decides.

In this chapter it became clear that new wave Clients are emerging, and this will demand radical changes in the services and skills of their advertising agencies. And moreover ...

- Three decades, the 1960s through to the 1980s, saw agencies more and more specialise in TV and the press. A capable and increasingly strong marketing services industry grew up behind them. This led to the battle of the budget, a phenomenon which defied the Client's best interest.

- Total quality marketing, in its aim to focus on relationships, requires the return of the one-stop shop, but this time with highly developed skills, an integrated marketing agency.

- Agencies do not have a good track record of impartiality and unbiased advice. Clients may decide to take their strategic counselling to more impartial advisers. Benefit in this instance will derive from involving the agency in the work of developing the strategy.

- Integration will become the most important goal of agencies. Clients who find satisfactorily integrated services available will use new methods to apportion the work; one of the most effective ways will be through appointing them guardians of a relationship, thus harmonising the objectives of both organisations.

- Marketing work will become increasingly specialised in the three areas which recognise the three types of Customer: prospective, existing and lapsed.

- Customer service teams face two options: the first is to increase manpower to provide a better Customer/servicer ratio. However, this is usually only capable of cosmetic, short-term gains. The second option is to rationalise the sales and marketing forces in the same way as the new agencies. This method provides powerful, sensitive marketing with integrity of corporate voice.

- Companies with a marketer at the top or where a pro-marketing environment exists on the board will make these changes fastest and will steal a valuable march on their competition.

15

New Objectives For Marketing

Quality marketing is different from quantity marketing. It's harder for a start. It requires greater degrees of professionalism, better use of intelligence, more understanding and more information.

Providing the information is perhaps the easiest part of all of those – databases to the rescue! However, professionalism, intelligence and understanding require not only that we do our job better, but that we do a better job. In other words, the new quality ethos must attach to both what we do and the way that we do it. This means it is essential that we build quality through defined objectives in both those areas. Conventional management techniques already provide us with the means to achieve these ends.

The major channels which will help us to boost quality will be our personnel-selection processes, training, the correct formulation of job specifications, corporate or departmental structures, and the reward and appraisal systems. Four of these in particular will be powerful in effective refocusing for quality goals. They are selection, training, structures and reward systems; the latter two so much so that you will find them covered in more detail in Chapters 21 and 22. However, the accent that quality places on recruitment and training needs thought in two contexts.

Quality loves people people

'People who need people are the luckiest people in the world', the song goes. And it's absolutely true. If you're looking to create an environment which cultivates relationships, you will have to ensure that you have the right people up front. Yet so often in life you find a dragon as your doctor's receptionist. These are people who seem to confuse *officious* with *efficient*. They build up defences against Customers. You see them in department stores, restaurants, and in countless of the classic hierarchies. Yet, buried in the throbbing heart of many corporate epicentres, you often find a one-man dynamo: a person who knows everyone, likes everyone, talks to everyone, makes friends with everyone, and who seems to be the social catalyst of the whole building. This is the natural person to be out front making friends of the Customers.

It is more necessary than ever to consider each person's ability to relate to people as a criterion in their work, which will, after all, be the business of building and managing relationships. This is not simply the question of smiling, being nice and saying the right thing, although that seems to give many businesses a hard enough problem. It is a question of understanding the Customer, looking at the longer term and creating the kind of atmosphere in which trust, loyalty, respect and even affection can develop. The chemistry between the individuals will be more vital, the closer and longer the relationship becomes.

The impact on recruitment here is clear; we must seek out and favour the kinds of people who can do that best. And, for those many companies in the process of restructuring, breaking down their hierarchies and flattening out, this is a hard task. The temptation in such cases is to take the middle management and redeploy them at the front end, thus, as IBM have done, increasing the number of people available to deal with Customers in one context or another. Yet the fact is that many people who have been obsessed, sometimes for years, with the internal workings of the company may have become corporate introverts; that is to say, the corporation, to whose welfare they have been dedicated for so long, assumes greater importance to them than the well-being or goodwill of the Customer.

Consider how this affects them. For example, if you look at the difference in approaches towards a late payer between someone in the accounts department and someone on the sales team, you'll appreciate my comment. One sees the Customer as a lawbreaker dedicated to withholding money which rightly belongs to his employer and which causes cash-flow problems; the other is trying to tread on eggshells, knowing he has to get the money in, but not wanting to risk the next order by raising awkward subjects or by threatening. Neither one is wrong; and yet they both are. They have to get the money in. So it is in both cases, right objectives, wrong mentality.

In relationship building the attitude of the individuals towards the Customer is critical. To some extent, this can be dealt with by training, but, inevitably, one is also looking for the actual capacity and propensity within that individual to relate to other human beings – Customers, the most important kinds of human being there are! Thus, we learn that quality starts with quality people –

quality, not just in the sense of how they perform against conventional targets, but how well they perform in their human interactions; how good they are at building and sustaining working relationships.

Effectively, all of this tells you that many of the staff you would ideally like to redeploy while restructuring may not have the necessary people skills, even though they have experience of your business in abundance. People skills can be enhanced by training, but they cannot successfully be implanted or bestowed on someone who just doesn't have them in the first place. If somewhere cannot be found for such people where they will not be damaging or inhibiting, they must be assisted in moving on to new pastures.

Increased training levels

The biggest problem for sales and marketing people in these new flatter structures is that the training ground (previously training was acquired in climbing the corporate hierarchy) has disappeared just at a time when the new objectives require even greater levels of training.

Thus, it will be important to ensure that workloads and timetables leave adequate time for training and education; that the resources, facilities and budget are available; and that the motivation is there for the training to be accepted and adopted by those who participate.

Relationships, not transactions

To a great extent, quantity objectives have forced marketing to become a business which concentrates on trying to create a number of transactions. The new desire is to establish the requisite number of relationships, which will, in turn, create the sales throughput. Thus, if your marketing is to become quality marketing, you will have to understand that your work must create the means for such relationships to grow and prosper, and to result in transactions. Understanding how this affects your business is important. Look at the locations, the atmosphere, the staff, the facilities and the circumstances in which your Customers will find themselves and question whether you have created a forum for transactions or relationships. Also, take a look at the processes and techniques you use. For example, how do you use sales promotion? Many marketers find that the more aggressive the techniques used in generating new Customer transactions, the less substantial the business generated. Let's consider this along with some other interesting facts ...

What makes advertising work?

While considering the new objectives of the marketer, let us not become totally obsessed with quality. Let's think about quantity too. In direct marketing, the media and style of so many campaigns enable you to test quite scientifically, and indeed quite economically, all manner of variations to see which perform best. However, on discovering this, lots of advertisers get quite carried away and start testing very trivial variants such as the colour of the letter signature – which in most cases will make no difference at all, or so little it is barely perceptible. They soon learn the result of experience! This tells you that big things make big differences and little things make little differences. Aha! But what is a big thing? In the creative category, for example, I, like many other direct marketers, proved conclusively many years ago that advertisement headlines generally work better under photographs than above them. Yet, strangely, the advertising industry persists, as it has for years, in preferring the reverse notion.

One particularly interesting set of statistics, which I use as a discussion point in many conferences, is that gathered by a leading, international, direct marketing agency through a most comprehensive analysis it carried out. The agency was trying to establish which factors most affected response rates and in what proportions. Here are its findings:

FACTORS AFFECTING RESPONSE
Response device	–	20%
Creativity	–	35%
Timing	–	100%
The offer	–	200%
The list	–	500%

I understand these figures were gained by measuring the best and worst situations. Thus, for example, if a mailing with a badly conceived reply device would pull an index of 100, and a mailing identical but with a good device, 120, the result was a response uplift of 20 per cent. The results were taken from many, many efforts, and the agency concerned was convinced of the validity of the results. To be clear about its findings, the first figure suggests that you will get a response improvement of typically 20 per cent (i.e. from, say 2 to 2.4 per cent) simply by thoughtful and informed attention to detail on the reply card or response device you are using. From experience, I know this to be so; and those in the financial services or insurance fields, where applications tend to be quite long and complex, will also know this to be the case.

The next one down, however, is something of a poser. Can it really be true that the total difference between indifferent and stunning creativity should be just 35 per cent? Whenever I discuss this with creative teams they either take umbrage or just don't believe this figure. It does take a little while for creative sensitivities to work it through. Yet it is interesting that, according to these figures, correct timing is almost exactly three times more important than the creative work. Perhaps many sales people will find that one easy to relate to. Yet the offer or proposition is a remarkable six times more powerful at making the advertising effective than is the creative aspect. To be fair, especially in the direct marketing context, many would argue that the two are inextricably woven together. However, when you think of the number of advertisements which carry a message but don't make a proposition or offer, it is easy to see how underrated this simple concept is.

The last figure is really very interesting; it suggests that finding the right audience for your ad is two and a half times more effective than the proposition, five times more critical than timing, and an astounding 15 times more important than the creative. This surely must question the current method of choosing an ad agency and the enormous priority given to creative skills in the selection process. On the face of it, here we see the relevance of an agency's abilities in the creative process reduced to a mere also-ran.

How do you choose your agency?

Rather than keep fellow proponents of the creative discipline in misery, let me say straightaway that the figures lie! There's more to it than meets the eye.

Yet before we burst the balloon, let us ponder a while on what I consider to be a most significant thinking point here. When pitching for business, agencies are rarely asked to give more than a cursory rundown of their media, strategic or planning skills. Because it's the most fun, and to many the most interesting, absorbing and entertaining, creativity rules. So in case the following should be thought to be dashing to the rescue of creativity, may I also make the plea for true weighting to be given to the other skills. Important as creativity is, it is certainly not all-important.

Creativity works to more than the sale

The catch, if that is what you can call it, in the figures is that they relate, in direct marketing terms, to what actually affects the response – and the response alone. They place no value at all on the pure advertising effect of the campaigns. Since most direct marketing and certainly most classical advertising have effect on brand and corporate values, which, of course, are largely to the credit of creativity, we must generally give it a better rating than 35 per cent suggests. However, I feel obliged to say that, in my experience, this is none the less one of the most overpriced and wasteful areas of the marketing world and needs a great deal of tightening up. For, at the end of the day, as Raymond Rubicam, co-founder of Young and Rubicam and one of the founding fathers of the international agency scene, once so succinctly put it, 'The object of advertising is to sell goods. It has no other justification worth mentioning.' Effectively, that statement, although made a few years ago, remains true; however, with the increased value that total quality marketing places on brand and corporate strength and loyalty building, we will once again see greater strategic and tactical emphasis placed on these aspects of marketing.

Creating sales that stick

I've always been a great believer in the idea that a first sale is only complete when the second sale is set up. If you feel the same way, you may have experienced a phenomenon which is well accepted in direct marketing and well known but rather less frequently worried about in selling.

The more promotion you use to close a sale, firstly, the higher the incidence of the sale failing to complete as Customers cancel (or perhaps gather the courage or self-resolve to withdraw); secondly, the more worries, complaints and attempts to retract you get during the 'buyer's remorse' period; and, thirdly, the less likely it is that the Customer will proceed to a second or third sale, eventually leading to optimum lifetime values.

On a rather pedantic technical note, it should be said that some direct marketers would argue that a 'flimsy', low-commitment first sale is better than no sale since it gives the opportunity to create a more solid basis through the ensuing dialogue. This could be generally correct. However, the point to which I would like to draw particular attention is that the logic for the phenomenon also holds a moral. The more manipulated Customers have been to pressure the sale through, the less receptive they are to the second approach. Moreover, companies that adopt heavy or continuous, highly promotional methods tend to attract the kind of Customer who responds to them. By definition, these will often be the kind of 'scavengers' who have less loyalty to give and who, therefore, will be more easily moved on by a better offer or bigger discount from anyone else. These people can collect premiums, gifts, and incentives like squirrels gather nuts.

If your business survives on such people and can stand the cost of marketing to them or can sustain the high level of expensively gained conquest business, then this will not trouble you. If you want to practise total quality marketing and be in the business of building sales through building relationships, you will appreciate that less will make more in the end. Exploitative processes can be used occasionally to great effect. But the same 'goodies' used to tempt the less likely into buying will often be more effective used as loyalty rewards or benefits.

Apples don't grow on companies

When you consider how to add quality to your organisation's marketing, it needs to be appreciated that marketing businesses and apple trees don't have too much in common. Apple trees can regularly produce quantity and quality. Businesses have been obsessed with the delivery of quantity for so long that quality goals will cause them stress and require much effort and commitment from all concerned. However, the return of quality objectives to marketing yields a benefit for the company which becomes a real treasure chest of an asset. By using its quality marketing process three ways it engenders stable, durable relationships which, enhanced by quality products and services, will lock Customers, staff and suppliers together around the corporate core.

When one decides to incorporate such objectives, they must be built in on a formal basis which enables success to be monitored and analysed. Although many of these objectives will be philosophical and cultural, it is still essential that they can be controlled and measured.

In thinking about the new objectives of the marketer we have considered the following points:

- Total quality marketing is harder than conventional quantity marketing. It seeks greater professionalism, intelligence, understanding of the Customer and information. Of these, information may prove the easiest to achieve through the use of database solutions.

- Quality-building systems, techniques and procedures must affect both what we do and the way we do it. This will place greater needs on, and challenge conventions in relation to, staff recruitment and selection, training resources, structures and reward systems.

- Quality marketing practices place increased values on the human interaction, chemistry and involvement since they are less focused on the generation of transactions and more on the construction of relationships.

- Companies who are restructuring to provide increased levels of Customer involvement should bear in mind when redeploying staff that they will need people skills in abundance.

- New flatter company structures, missing the hierarchical ascension, have effectively gained much, but have lost a valuable training ground with a proven track record which has been used since time immemorial. Thus, replacement training opportunities and resources must be made available.

- Marketers must create forums in which to do business which cultivate relationships rather than simply generate transactions.

- In the above respect, marketers will need to adjust their objectives to require less promotion and build more solid business. A business that uses exploitation processes attracts a less loyal type of Customer who can be more easily tempted away by others. Quality marketers enjoy longer-lasting, more profitable and more satisfying relationships with their Customers.

- In choosing ad agencies, the value of creativity in generating business is less than in image-, corporate- and brand-building. When selecting an agency, its ability to identify and reach markets is increasingly valuable. However, the value of the creative input will continue as the need for more loyalty to the brand and the company increases.

- Companies who appreciate and use total quality marketing concepts build Customer loyalty as an asset for their business. However, to succeed in implementing quality techniques, companies must be sure that they are adopted on a formal basis and that such new cultural and philosophical objectives are set, monitored, analysed and rewarded.

16

The Shift in Selling Style

I predicted earlier that the practice of selling has a lot of change to make; however, in writing this chapter, I am aware it's subject needs to be sensitively handled. There is a danger that many groups of salespeople might be alienated because they interpret the comments I am about to make as, at best critical; at worst, offensive. This would be quite contradictory to my aim, since it might fuel a sales-versus-marketing conflict of thought which it is vitally important should not arise.

However, there are changes already taking place which dictate a change in selling style. I will do my best to explain how I see this affecting the way selling happens. It is left to the vision of individuals concerned to determine whether and how they might wish to adapt for the future. None the less, I am proposing new ways which I believe will be more effective. By implication, the proposal of new methods often criticises the old ones; in this case that is true. The old ways were appropriate for their time, a point which may become clearer when you consider the three generations of selling.

At first glance, to a salesperson who has matured during the 1970s and 1980s especially, this view of the future might seem a little lacking in aggression. Again that's true. The sales style that goes with total quality marketing is softer. It is assertive rather than aggressive; anxious to serve the company's own best interests through serving its Customer; accepting that the rewards take longer to build, but are greater when they come.

Although I describe the selling style as softer, I would point out again that quality selling methods, just like quality marketing methods of which they are part, are harder to achieve. They require long-term commitment from the top and selfless dedication to the Customer by all the individuals concerned.

To be clear, I am not suggesting that all salespeople and organisations will change to these new methods. I expect to see plenty of all three generations around in the future. However, I expect the new style to predominate over the time span which this book covers. But some organisations will prefer to stay with the methods they know, the familiar ways that have served them well. Others will move ahead with time, learning the newer, more caring processes and appreciating the stability and value this will add to their company, their career, and their life. However, I do expect Customers to prefer the newer methods and this may indeed provide the greatest impetus for change.

The three generations of selling

As you look back over the past decades, perhaps remembering some of the strategies which we saw in Tables 8.1, 8.2 and 8.3 covering that time on pages 80–1, it becomes clear that the business of selling did not escape the helter-skelter down the quantity route. In fact, during the eras of mass production and mass marketing, it would be fair to say that selling was in the front line. As the quantity target pressures built up, it was the refinement of sales techniques and promotion – the ability to manipulate markets and exploit sales opportunities to a greater degree – which carried both the greatest workload and the greatest responsibility. It was not uncommon in many companies to see the marketing department reduced from its strategic and principled role, to a mere inventor of constant merchandising, promotional and incentive programmes. It is no wonder that the infamous idea of marginal costing sprang to popularity in these times.

These were days when the Customer is king concept was a means to an end, the end being the heavily disguised truth that the product was actually king. When you glance down the 1960s column on Table 8.1 you can clearly see the facts there: a growth mission for all products; random product lines and products; competing on product features; pricing based on cost; generalised sales forces; heavy advertising and hard selling. But look at the line 1.2 which starts 'Product Orientation', becoming 'Market Orientation' developing to 'Customer/Competitor/Channel Orientation'. So be it!

The first generation of selling

As we move through the 1990s, any lingering doubt that we live in a 'benefits' society will fade. We buy things for what they do for our lifestyle. In the 1960s and early 1970s we were deeply embedded in a 'features' society. The ads for cars carried checklists inviting you to compare feature for feature. We switched from black-and-white TV to the newly featured colour. In the 20 postwar years across the world we came from scarce availability to overloaded markets groaning with products that needed pumping down the distribution channel with great effort and energy. Eventually many markets moved into glut. The consumer revelled as prices dropped, and gradually we saw the two-car family, a TV in several rooms, and dishwashers. It could well be argued that what I describe as the first generation of selling was not actually the first at all. It developed during the age of glut; a natural evolution from the heavy-advertising, heavy-selling time. I call it the first generation beause it was the predecessor of the following generations, as surely as ape preceded man.

In searching for a word to describe the style of selling of this era, the word 'muscular' comes to mind and seems to fit admirably. To be sold to was almost to be press-ganged. Lessons in selling were given by guru figures to hundreds of avaricious life assurance salesmen who worshipped them as if they were indeed some new god. These figures were masters of their universe, kings of the silver tongue and the smooth psychology that left a Customer with no more 'No's'. So the only result was 'Yes'. Conquest. The commission register rings up another sale.

The language of this generation was aggressive and, in its literal sense, offensive. They 'attacked' a market. Their whole *modus operandi* was military. Of course, it led to some jolly good annual sales conferences. Great praise was heaped upon the salesperson who browbeat the most Customers and sold the most goods. But nobody stopped to think how the Customer felt about all this. Why bother? The sale was everything; the commission cheque mere confirmation that winning the great sales race was what life was all about.

It was all very simple in the days of the first generation. You sold product and people bought its production; or if you were a consumer, its features. We bought lawn mowers because they cut lawns; pop-up toasters because they popped up; copiers because they copied; typewriters because they typed. Gradually, through the latter part of the 1970s and into the 1980s, a new generation was born.

The second generation of selling

This was the time when selling started to deal with the notion of added value. Those who learned that competitive discounting led to a war of attrition turned their attention to increasing Customer satisfaction and looking beyond the product.

The five-year warranty and extended service packages were invented. Computers came with programmes and games; televisions with infrared remotes. 'Have a nice day' came to Europe. Those who had bought copiers because they copied bought them now because they copied faster, collated, did back and front and plain paper, and came with a service contract. Those who had bought typewriters because they typed bought something entirely new. It was called a word processor. It was absolutely useless – unless, of course, you bought the added-value package. That gave you the equipment plus a training programme. And as a result, now, one word-processor operator could do the work of two or three typists. But only with the training.

Suddenly, the added-value age was upon us. It sold the product but with the skills that helped you get the best out of it. Suddenly, what Customers were buying was no longer the product. It was increased productivity.

The selling style for this generation I call 'cupped hands'. For many consumers, added value brought the promise of better service. However, in this generation it was a fairly cosmetic operation. It culminated in the seed corn of the quality age. Hotels started to put photographs of their managment in their lobbies. Name badges became the order of the day. Barclays Bank allowed its tellers to smile. The shopping mall was discovered in Europe. The Customer mistook this patronising lip service to service for the real thing and was momentarily content. Hip organisations trained their telephonists to answer 'Good Morning. Thank you for calling the Hayling Island Post House. Sharon speaking. How may I help you?' Telephone companies announced record profits! The Customer service campaign – the non-thinking man's answer to 'in search of excellence' – was underway. However, the thinking man was at work looking into total quality management, the first step in true recognition of the move away from goals geared uniquely to quantity.

Yet, as we have found already, we will not be going backwards so far to the future that product superiority or perfection will be enough. The time for marketing to take the lead is with us.

The third generation of selling

It had to happen. If you return again to the 1990s columns of Tables 8.1, 8.2 and 8.3 on pages 80–1, you can see the evidence stacking up before you:

- niche or customised marketing;
- implementation excellence;
- Customer/competitor/channel evaluation;
- product-line rationalisation;
- strategic mission for each product;
- multiplexed salesforce;
- competing on quality, design and service;
- priced against Customers' perceived value;
- the product of strategic alliances.

We're undoubtedly heading through the age of individualisation back to relationship values. But beware, for in both the consumer and business markets, the Customers expectation has changed, and so, to a degree, has what they're out there buying.

Take the business market. In previous generations we saw the typewriter become the word processor; and we saw how it was the skills that went with that which gave it the added value of increased productivity for the Customer. Here, in the third generation, the seller and the buyer join together to decide what the buyer needs and how best it can be supplied. Thus, the company who sold the word processor would now sit down with its Customer to decide together how the seller's skills can best be made to work together to fill the buyer's needs for the future.

Thus, our word-processor manufacturer might find out that his Client, a publisher, is looking to computerise his typesetting so that it can run from keyboarding as raw journalistic input, be scanned and edited by a third party, and then be moved down the line to typesetting and page make-up and on again to print. The publisher is thus looking to buy the seller's know-how – the equipment or hardware becoming a secondary part of the whole process.

Table 16.1: The three generations of selling

PHASE	TECHNIQUE	WHAT YOU SELL	WHAT THEY BUY
FIRST GENERATION	Selling	The product	Production
SECOND GENERATION	Added-value selling	The product with skills	Productivity
THIRD GENERATION	Multi-discipline marketing	Know-how (opportunity)	Ideas (opportunity)

Is what you are selling what people want to buy?

For more and more markets, the product is becoming a know-how product. Oddly, since know-how is being sold and ideas, therefore, are being bought, it seems to me that finally selling's evolutionary process has arrived at a conclusion where, possibly in many markets, the two have become the same for the very first time. Both represent opportunity. That is what is being sold and that is what is being bought.

This concept of know-how as a product is fast gaining recognition in many business markets and in certain consumer markets such as financial services. It has an irrefutable logic. Which makes more sense to you? Consider the choices:

1. the machine itself – a first-generation product;

2. the machine tailored to your specification or with the added value of skill opportunities to get the best out of it;

3. the machine designed to do a better job for you tomorrow because it was the result of a team effort by the brains at the buying company with the brains at the manufacturer?

So this is the first part of the age of individualisation where the third generation of selling excels. Yet individualisation promises more – it promises recognition, a level of personal service which is both enticing and captivating.

The new strength of the retailer

It is this area, the highly personalised, all-embracing service, that I see as being the big growth area for the retailer of the future. Again, like so many aspects of TQM, it requires courage and conviction to commit yourself to it as a direction.

A Mintel report, 'Retailing and the Shopper' produced at the gateway to the 1990s, looked specifically at the UK but drew some conclusions which can certainly be projected into 'Western' Europe and, in some respects, almost globally. The Mintel report foresaw that the 1990s would see a dramatic return in the high streets and shopping malls of better choice, service and quality. A director, Frank Fletcher, was quoted as saying that 'In the 1980s the Customer has been King in name only. But the consumer can still only buy what the retailers let them.' A pretty powerless king! He continued, 'In the 1990s, the stores that truly make the Customer King will be the stores that succeed. Life will not be easy for the retailer ... who will have to work very hard indeed to persuade shoppers to part with their money.' A problem exacerbated no doubt by the richer, more affluent, and well-equipped consumer facing a boring row of parity products and having less real need to spend.

This promises an interesting trend back to the smaller, specialist or expert retailer who can demonstrate a discernible difference through choice or through service, providing a very definite arena for relationships rather than transactions.

Do retailing and niche marketing go together?

This is an interesting question to which I have no doubt whatsover that the answer is 'yes'. However, the larger and more widespread the retailer's product range, the more difficult niche marketing would appear to be. This is a fallacy, probably most widely spread by a common misunderstanding of the term *niche marketing*.

I won't embarrass the rather well-known business commentator and marketing columnist by naming him, but he was none the less the author of a quite searing indictment of the concept of niche marketing in retailing. As the UK groaned its way through the 'ghost' recession of 1990 (Mrs Thatcher kept assuring everyone, including both her chancellors of that year, that there wasn't one which might have contributed to her downfall!), this columnist pointed out the extraordinary risk of niche marketing to any retailers considering what he felt to be a step in the most 'overrated and hazardous' direction. His evidence, had it been in favour of the right argument, would have been compelling. He pointed to the demise or hard times of the small but ubiquitous Sock Shop, Tie Rack, Knickerbox, Paperchase, and Cookie Kiosks.

Speciality retailing and niche marketing are at opposite ends of the spectrum. One takes a 'niche product', as it were, and places it before an unsegmented market (save for the outlet locations); the other, through one means or another, identifies or targets a small homogeneous group of consumers and develops products or services that meet the needs of that group in relation to the common factors that make up the homogeneity.

The speciality retailers that suffered most are likely to be those that failed to niche-market and therefore, when hard times hit, were unable to consolidate their major or frequent buyers around them because they had made no effort whatsover to get to know them or even simply to identify them. Thus, they could not materially reduce their resources without similarly reducing their market exposure and consequent sales.

Retailers who have already demonstrated a great ability to segment internally and backwards through product groups and departmental thinking, must for the future examine and practise the methods of Customer group and individual thinking.

There is an interesting side issue which stems from the failure of speciality retailers to appreciate the wider benefits of marketing and the consequent strength and resilience marketing could have added instead of leaving them so vulnerable. The issue, or rather question, raised is why investors find such high-risk businesses so attractive. My belief is that the City is using outdated methods to assess sales and marketing capabilities from an investor's point of view and may thus have become a little naive and vulnerable itself.

The large and multinational retailers must about turn. They have become obsessed with asserting their strength over the manufacturers. This has resulted in the biggest example of cutting of one's nose to spite one's face the business world has ever seen. It has pushed many retailers throughout the world into a price-cutting syndrome coupled with an overuse of advertising and promotions. This, in turn, has backfired on the consumer and the manufacturer. The manufacturer has found his margins squeezed, has lost control of his business and is unable to invest sufficiently in quality and product development. The consumer has been given less choice, less service, and poorer value.

The third generation of selling, building relationships with Customers and treating suppliers as partners is a mix which will return the retail world to its correct perspective, and will mean enjoying the cost-saving benefit of long-lasting, stable, loyal relationships with its Customers and working together with its manufacturers and suppliers to meet the increasingly demanding requirements of its Customers. This will place the Customer back as the centre of attention; give the retailer back his ability to serve and provide individually tailored advice and counsel; and enable the manufacturers to regain control over their margins and thereby restore the investment levels to their optimum. I wonder who has the courage to do it first?

The large multiple retailers in Europe and, to some extent, in the US have set themselves up. They increased the Customer's perception of price as a factor in purchasing and suffered ultimately because of it. Now, as the world outside retailing moves toward quality and vastly increased levels of priority for Customer service and Customer care, retailing, bereft of sufficient margin, will have to rethink its position or be out of step with the communities upon whom it relies.

As we related this and other ideas to the shift in selling style, we saw that:

- Selling is entering a time of softer style than has been used for 30 years or more.

- The three generations of selling tracked the styles through time and identified know-how as a major new 'product' for the future.

- Certain retailers in Europe and the US may suffer because of their obsession with controlling their suppliers rather than committing themselves to caring for their Customers.

17

The Changes in Buying

We have learned that Customers will become more demanding. We have learned that they will be looking for better service, better Customer care, and a more individual approach to both the handling of their business and the products and services that are offered to them. Yet, if we are going to see a time shortly when the Customers rule, how will this manifest itself? What precisely will they expect? What will we have to do to get their custom in the age of total quality marketing.

Of course, each Customer will react differently. Each market sector may react differently. Particular countries will retain, possibly even increase, their national idiosyncrasies. Yet it is still possible to predict in general the ways that buying and selling will change. That is the subject of the next two chapters; we'll take the buying process first.

The environment to which we are changing is itself an environment of change; frequent, indeed relentless, change for businesses whatever their markets. And while we cope and learn to deal with all this change and the new demands of our Customers, we must also address the fact that we have to deliver more intimate relationships, individual recognition and satisfaction, and that Customers will require to be understood.

So what are the demands?

In some ways all the changes in buying explained here could be seen as increasing demands. However, I feel there are four particular areas where there will be heightened expectation of marketing by Customers.

Firstly, our Customers will undoubtedly adopt more and new communications media as they become available. And in this electronic age one should expect new media to proliferate. I anticipate that this will happen faster within the business community. Yet, having said that, I must add that there is also a widely held belief that we will see a vast increase in those 'in-between' businesses, namely freelance or independent consultants and specialists, many of whom operate from home or from practices and work in effective but small teams. Certainly, if you look at the de-massification and restructuring going on, coupled with the need to stay flexible and the increase of know-how as a product, you can understand the logic and therefore the prediction. It simply means that the advice given earlier for marketing directors, that it's better to have a big budget than a big department, may stand up just as well for other business disciplines too. There is also a widely held feeling that the training industry will, as it tries to cope with the vast new levels required of it, show massive growth in the same smaller consultancies.

However, it would be foolish to think that these media changes will occur only in the business markets. The consumer too will view the proliferation in a different way. Here it is likely they will see it as choice. Therefore, businesses who deal with the consumer markets will need to add the new media and communications opportunities to their range in order to satisfy the wider band of users they have.

The second category of increased demand is that of access to know-how and specialists. One of the effects that IBM appreciated as it restructured was the wealth of know-how and information which had previously been lost, locked up in the hierarchy, unseen and unavailable to its Customers. As IBM flattened out and moved these experienced people to positions where they came in touch with the Customer and his need, it released a value for the company and for its Customers which had never been exposed before.

Thirdly, I believe that Customers will seek more information from their suppliers, and less data, although it may be that this demand will be satisfied through the partnership style of relationship, and therefore become a mutual development process. However, in general, the point remains the same. Customers will expect specialists and knowledge workers to be in the thick of it with them, rather than at a distance, say, at the corporate base.

Fourthly, corporately and individually, with the relationship increasing expectations of loyalty, commitment and enthusiasm on both sides, Customers will expect nothing short of devotion. I described it earlier as heart, mind and soul.

Inevitably, these four heightened demand levels will need a medium through which they can be delivered and satisfied. That, of course, is the relationship itself. So next we turn to the

Customer's expectation of that relationship. How will it change? In a word, intimately.

Going for more intimate relationships

As the spotlight is turned onto the human interaction, relationships will become more personal and less corporate. Teams will become partners in problem-solving, so there will develop three teams, in effect: the buying team, the selling team and the combined team. Actually I prefer to drop the buying and selling terms, finding the words 'commissioner and marketer' more appropriate. This often causes me to be accused of going too far!

Thus, also, within this more intimate style, we see that the marketer must be more educated and informed about the buyer, his company, systems and processes, and markets. In turn, the marketer will be expected to use these changes to the benefit of the buyer. For example, in the field of service expectancy, four categories can be identified where we can anticipate major demand spirals. These are:

1. improved stock/availability;

2. better distribution;

3. faster delivery/reaction time;

4. more customisation.

It can be appreciated at once that there appear some paradoxes even in these four areas; improved stock appears to fight with customisation. But they exist none the less.

The need to be understood

As the amount of automation, technology and computing increases, the market will constantly remind us that the building of satisfactory relationships has its practical and material dimensions, but is first and foremost an exercise in human chemistry, dynamics and interaction.

Customers will ask us to understand them as the individual people they are and treat them accordingly. This has two particular aspects. Firstly, we must understand that behind their demands on us lies a simple desire on their part to meet the demands of their marketplace, and, secondly, we must understand the pressures they work under. How can we help take that pressure off; or at least, help them to handle it? How should we adapt or adjust what we do to take account of it.

I ask my audiences, 'What will be the biggest hurdle for executives and managers in the future?' It's a revealing process! One popular answer is 'getting to grips with technology'; but by far the most common fear voiced is that of stress, a problem which takes a mounting toll. Handling and dealing with people in a normal state can be a complex and interesting business. When almost the whole business world is witnessing the record levels of stress which are still climbing, then this will require more understanding still. Stress, incidentally, is just one more unwanted by-product of the quantity age.

For the future, Customers will not so much expect us just to supply or serve them. They will involve us in their planning; they will ask us to take part in their education and training processes; they will expect us to put our know-how together with theirs; and they will expect us to help them master technology.

For the consumer marketers, such as FMCG, some of these demands may not seem to relate directly. How, you may ask, can you be more understanding of Customers? How can you have more intimate relationships? How can you adopt new media, communications and technology? If you really remain unsure, go back to the supermarket example in Chapter 4. Yet, for FMCG brand owners – and many others – there are two Customers: their retailers and their end-user/buyers. How to meet the demands we have discussed here for a retailer is quite easy; but what about the end-user? Here the brand owners must look at the qualities they bestow upon the brand and the way they position it. Futhermore, they must look at their opportunities to partner their retailers and build loyalty to mutual benefit. Where retailers insist on sole ownership of the Customer, brand owners can resort to other means to increase Customer service and care, and through this begin the gradual process of relationship building. However, they must always remember that, unless they radically alter their distribution channel, the intermediary may have more, and often very damaging, power, over the consumer.

In this chapter, we have looked at some of the changes in buying criteria and expectations. We know that the Customer's changing perception of value will be of increasing significance in many areas and price less so. However, we also considered that the changes in buying will raise Customer's expectations and that they will require:

- *satisfaction of new demands*
    1. more communications, new technology, new media
    2. greater access to specialists and know-how
    3. more information, less data
    4. devotion of mind, body and soul;
- *more intimate relationships*
    1. more personal, less corporate
    2. more educated and informed
    3. more reactive to needs
    4. higher service expectancy
       a) improved stock/availability/reaction time
       b) better distribution
       c) faster delivery
       d) more customisation;
- *the need to be understood*
    1. empathise with the human dynamics
    2. recognise demands and pressures
    3. share growth path
    4. assist education and training
    5. help master technology.

18

The Changes in Selling

As we have shown, the changes in selling are far reaching. Undoubtedly, the most influential factor behind these changes is the switch from transaction-based work to relationship-based work.

When our objectives change to include quality objectives, they will place in front of all others the strategy of building solid and stable growth for the corporation through these broad-based, long-term relationships. In order to provide a safe and trusting atmosphere for that relationship to flourish, there are some ground rules, some changes to conventional thinking. For example, I expect both parties to make each other quite openly aware of the financial, material and intellectual dynamics. There will be a shared understanding, a mutual respect for the desire to embark down a planned profit-development path.

Marketing is a flexible and reactionary process. Marketers must constantly research and monitor their activities, and they must analyse and establish values and directions. On the basis of such analysis, marketers make decisions. This welding together of such practices behind the transactions within the relationship is a long-time procedure of the direct marketing fraternity and will become one of the most satisfying and rewarding processes for the classical practitioners to adopt as marketing fusion takes place.

Also, marketing is now segment or niche orientated. We have seen duality, the apparent dichotomy of global branding while markets fragment and de-massify. Let us now examine the changes in 'selling' practices, which, in general, will become more 'marketing' in style.

Building secure relationships works for both sides

Moving away from transaction-led selling, or, as I prefer to call it, exploitation selling, to satisfaction marketing pays much less attention and gives much lower priority to short-term, volume-sales missions. Now relationships are founded on the cornerstone engraved with the words 'Customer welfare'. Quite simply, we must dedicate ourselves to serving the Client's best interest on every level possible. Thus, we can identify the four corners of the world in which selling products and services through total quality marketing must operate, a cultural square where everything is bounded by quality, service, added-value and know-how. The mentality of the long-term relationship is one that requires that both parties share and are concerned about their own and each other's trends, threats and opportunities.

An important feature, or indeed asset, of these relationships is their longevity and security. The security, particularly, once created, breeds massive mutual confidence and commitment. This, in turn, creates valuable benefits in the quality and productivity of the work, but also provides a background against which risk-taking and major investment (not words I usually place too close together lest they mate!) are suitably encouraged.

A planned profit-development path

The trouble is that while change is hitting businesses so relent-lessly, chaos and havoc are waiting underneath lest they fall. This will require that business planning functions be modified to be less rigid; the area of planning is a prime area where we will witness the openness in dealings and discussions as profit-development paths are opened up. In order to encourage the necessary atmosphere, the future will see, what are by conventional standards, quite extra-ordinary exchanges of information from both sides. This will include:

● disclosure of personal and business goals;

● disclosure of detailed corporate growth and development plans;

● disclosure of personal and corporate reward, incentive and motivation potential.

Such kind of discussion and collaboration encourages exciting unity of purpose and comradeship; it is also very healthy for the 'third team effect'. Further, it correctly places the highest value on know-how as we accelerate into the third generation of selling. The structures required to facilitate such relationships and the working styles they encourage are, however, necessarily quite different from conventional hierarchies since a very much more broadside exposure is required to support and deliver these relationships. Yes, many differences are developing as we move away from the supply-and-demand style and towards mutual-interest projects.

Again, you will find these changes relate similarly to the consumer, especially, I suspect, the question of personnel remuneration and rewards, a point which will have dramatic impact on the future, as we will see in Chapter 21.

Marketing becomes analysis-based

Marketing already understands the value of certain kinds of research. However, the research industry throughout the world is becoming more innovative and experimental. This is just as well, for, marketing will need it to provide information which is wider and deeper – and it will need this information both faster and more frequently. As planning becomes less rigid in its outlook, the information on which it is based will need to be more adventurous and explorative in its scope, yet more reliable and sensitive in its delivery and interpretation.

Thus, future research work will enable us to make more intelligent value perceptions and thereby value judgements and, of course, decisions. These will, in turn, improve the quality, design and service aspects of our products.

Orientating for the niche

'People can be overselective in their market selection,' said the managing director. He is the dynamic head of a mail-order bookseller specialising in the business market. He went on to explain how a member of his team had analysed the sales of one book (let us invent one here, say, *How to be a Super Sales Manager*) and found that fewer than 1 in 20 of the buyers were sales managers. The rest were made up of a strange collection of sales and marketing people, small-business managing directors and even, somewhat inexplicably, a midwife! As a result, his company had found that what many other direct marketers would consider to be a hopelessly scatter-gun approach worked well. Basically, he suggested, the more people he let know about more books (of particular qualities and types, naturally), the more he sold.

This may be true for his company, but not for most marketers. It is actually not so much to do with the strange idiosyncrasies of his business, his Customers, his market, or his products. It is actually to do with the way he deals with his Customers and the opportunity he has to get to know and understand them. However, his business runs on classic direct marketing lines and has a single-dimension relationship with his Customers. And very successfully it works too. However, when you look at the take-it-or-leave-it, art gallery approach the retail book trade has adopted, this is no surprise. Moreover, getting to know the Customers can and should include building a picture of what they actually purchase, as against what their job title, business category, demographics or sociographics suggest they might want to buy.

To operate successfully in a niche market, you must develop a relationship which gets you nearer to the Customers; better able to meet more of their niche needs. Otherwise, you are simply headed the wrong way down a funnel. You end up with fewer people buying fewer or single highly specialist products. Niche marketing has to do with the ability to adapt (or abandon) hitherto mass-marketed, mass-produced items and to develop and tailor them (or create new) by adding value and specialisation to the smaller groups that make up your total market. What makes the groups smaller is the information you have about them and their needs. Thus, until my bookseller friend was ready to create individual relationships with his Customers, in the way that retail bookshops could, but usually don't, he would never have known that the midwife bought the book for her husband to celebrate his forth-coming promotion to sales manager.

Another aspect of niche marketing and the necessary relation-ships required to profit best from the concept is that it requires that the seller represent the full capability of the company to the buyer. This cuts across brands and across product ranges. What's more, niche orientation requires that, whatever we call our front-end array -- salesforce, business development team, account managers, marketing departments, outlets, branches -- their aims must reflect the relationship-building objectives. Their teams are structured according to the niche or niches they deal with. The only real conjecture here is how the force is structured to achieve this, the main topic of the following chapter.

Along with all this, indeed almost a catalyst to the evolution, is the availability of suitable database support for such market-ing structures. These facilitate the networking of information, the movement and transfer of data and the ability to adopt techno-creative marketing communications with the market, other teams, and necessary suppliers.

When you put together the content of these last two chapters, the changes in buying and the changes in selling, there is only one clear direction. It is the very same direction to which so many aspects of our future point: back to relationship-based quality marketing techniques. Also we have seen how the major ways in which the thinking and motivations of both sides of the marketing process will change. In selling these can be summed up as:

- *Building secure, long-term relationships*

    1. Customer welfare on all levels is the first priority.

    2. Security breeds confidence and commitment; it also increases investment and encourages exploration.

- *Creating planned profit-development paths*

    1. Mutual growth tracks for Customer and supplier.

    2. Openness about:
       a) personal and business goals;
       b) detailed corporate growth and development plans;
       c) personal and corporate reward, incentive and motivational potential.

- *Marketing increasingly analysis-based*

    1. Planning with less rigid boundaries increases the need for wider and deeper research, faster and more frequently provided.

    2. Research needs to be more adventurous and explorative in scope while being more reliable and sensitive in delivery and interpretation.

- *Orientating for the niche*

    1. Relationships are the media through which niche markets blossom and yield their maximum potential.

    2. Niche marketing requires the ability to move from mass-production to customised and tailored production *en masse*.

    3. What creates a niche is the information you have about the individuals or organisations and their needs; the more information, potentially the smaller the niches.

4. Niche marketing requires across-the-brand or across-the-product range selling. It flourishes when one-to-one communications are the order of the day.

5. The full potential of niche marketing is realisable through databases and the supporting software which enable the satisfactory operation of the optimum working structures and information networking.

19

Granular Marketing

There has been inference of and reference to marketing department structures at several times throughout this book. I also have used the phrase 'backwards to the future' and other similar phrases a number of times, the message being that, in many ways, the total quality marketing gospel is not new. It is as old as the hills and well tried and proven. This is undeniable fact. Although, like world wars, thank goodness (and, in the case of the latter, let us pray it stays that way), those who can recall what it was really like are growing fewer in number. For most marketers, it is pure hearsay – or at least it would have been except for the fact that the true standards and values of the quality regime in marketing have been so shunned and spurned for so long, that they have been neither heard nor said.

We have already seen how quantity took over and how and why the pendulum swung so ridiculously far the other way. It is no wonder the consumer is feeling that enough is enough. I suppose the question here, then, is why we can't turn back the clock and market like they used to in, what can quite fairly in this context be described as, the good old days. What has changed? The answer is nearly everything. The whole dynamics of marketing are entirely different: the numbers, the speed with which things are required, the expectations of Customers generally have changed out of all perspective. Moreover, as their just compensation for the exploitation they have suffered, Customers will expect the wrongs to be righted but to hang on to the 'rights' they have gained. The business world, too, is not made up of idealists and philanthropists; it will consider accepting the return of quality only as long as it can hang on to the quantity. I believe that both sides can, largely, win with total quality marketing. I also recognise that the corporate structures that delivered quality the last time round would collapse under the strain as we pumped today's quantities into the system. Unfortunately, making them bigger or more robust will not help either since they are too unwieldy to provide the speed and reactions required in today's business world. Indeed, with flexibility as a keyword to survival for the future, this point could be well taken by so many of today's businesses who still operate the same elaborate hierarchies and command and control systems that they operated at the turn of the last century. The systems have not been built to provide quality and quantity. They have only succeeded with one or the other. So there is a strong argument to look for new ways.

Is it necessary to meddle with corporate infrastructures to market quality?

Not necessarily. However, it is necessary to consider quite radical changes to the structures of sales and marketing. Yet this gives me a reservation about having one type of structure throughout the organisation and another in the marketing department. To a large extent, individual answers here will depend on the nature of the organisation, the nature of the business, and the way it interfaces with its markets.

Tracking back to the three generations of selling will help us to solve these issues. Consider the first generation and the structure of its sales and marketing division or departments. It has a classic hierarchical shape. From director to regional or branch sales and marketing managers to district sales or product managers through to the salesforce. These managers operate via the muscular regime. This creed is that to sell more you need more people to sell. Their operating methods are aggressive and highly promotional. Their objectives are single-minded – to move product. The salespeople work alongside a marketing team where, in the worst cases, a strong sales director will have beaten marketing into subservience, and they will have become a support group providing promotional and marketing services on demand. In the less severe cases, the sales and marketing teams do work together but without a great deal of respect on either side; and they don't always like each other very much!

From this we have discussed the evolutionary change which developed with the second generation of selling. The idea was to present a wider spread to the market. It cultivated operatives who had a Client service mission. This pattern was achieved through simple refocusing of direction and by closer integration of the sales and marketing effort. Indeed, this regime often became confused and argued about whose role started and ended where. Here is the 'cupped hands' regime at work. Its operating methods are caring and attentive and much more service orientated than its preceding generation. Its creed is service assistance; and its corresponding objective the added-value sale.

Ideas from advertising agencies

The mid-1970s to mid-1980s saw a global outbreak of these units, like daisies on an early summer lawn. I have always thought that advertising agencies set the best example of this type. Their account-handling structure – account executives, account managers, account group managers, account directors and account group directors – worked extremely well in the context of the big monolithic agency. However, there are danger points.

The first of these is the way the communications path gets longer as the organisation is successful and expands. A group with four account executives, two account managers and an account director can be expanded, with relative ease, to, say, eight account executives, four account managers, two account group managers and an account director. The problem here is that as the layers increase, the centres of inspiration and authority in such hierarchies, the leaders, are getting further and further apart. Thus, life becomes an inevitability of small decisions and procedures where major decision-making is tedious, cumbersome and slow.

The second danger point is a tendency to bureaucratic systems in response, usually, to the volatile, unpredictable and fast-moving nature of the people involved and the work they handle. Those bureaucracies can also become self-fulfilling, with heavy overheads and low productivity, hidden by the amount of work they generate in perpetuating their own existence. It is strange how often these units, in many senses a team, have little if any team spirit.

The sales or Customer-service units, when looked at in detail, are, in fact, simply microhierarchies within greater hierarchies, see Figure 19.1, below. Where they are headed by a strong, inspirational leader, they can be very successful. They tend to have supervisory and operational strata, the operational tier generally having three kinds of communications functionaries:

> The ambassador – a traveller
> The voice   – a telemarketer
> The scribe   – contact through the database

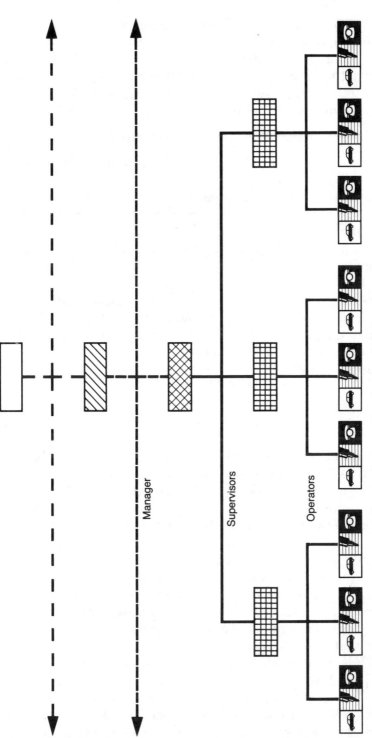

Manager

Supervisors

Operators

Figure 19.1 Customer-service units: hierarchies within hierarchies?

There have been massive developments here in databases, and sales-direction and management systems are now coupled to Customer communications and transactions by computer. This leads to all manner of cost-efficiency improvements, from increased control and management effectiveness to better stock control and resource management.

Is the classical Client service team concept dying?

The fact is that the classical Client service team concept can still work very well indeed. However, for the future, it will work best for those who have found their natural place in the second generation. It provides a perfectly practical answer for those who associate their needs or situation with those described under 'Option one: more people', in Chapter 14. However, the words I used in relation to that option were 'compromise' and 'cosmetic'. My belief is that we need to see a new style of Client service team being created, and I propose that such teams should work as granules within a broadside structure or a network structure, as we shall see shortly.

What style of teams work best?

It should be remembered, when choosing which business style will best suit the teams, that the more traditional methods and techniques will work better with the classical Client services team. It is, after all, a hierarchy. It is with the new flatter structures where new management styles flourish. Yet, in a hierarchy, rank, authority, and strict procedural ideas about control, transmission of instructions, and reporting thrive. This is not generally a good environment for experimentation and entrepreneurism.

Yet, in the context of individualised product and Customer service, together with a need for increased sensitivity and responsiveness, one can see why the reservations develop with conventional structures, techniques and management styles.

The new marketing management style for the third generation is responsible: it can take decisions and be accountable for them. The new style is mature: it understands the need to become more business orientated. The new style is autonomous, adventurous and challenging: it stands ready to get close to Customers, to find new ways to satisfy their demands, and it constantly questions beliefs, practices and dogma. The new marketing style is alert, free thinking, strategy conscious and technologically competent and fluent.

Getting closer to Customers

An important realisation of getting closer to Customers is that hitherto they have not known what they want because they have not known what they could have; they have simply taken the choices on offer. As the relationship succeeds and the boundaries fall, one of the greatest fields for new product ideas, development and proving will be within the project work that develops. When Customers get to appreciate the boundless choice available with customisation, I expect industrial, professional and commercial progress to speed up tenfold; this should occur by the turn of the millennium. The technology is already sufficient to support such a jump. It may even enable us to reach this level earlier still.

I'd like to interrupt myself at this point to explore some other side effects of customisation, since they will have great impact on the structure of the marketing department.

The knock-on effect of customisation (indeed, individualisation pushes this argument forward further still) is very substantial. One can predict a huge decrease in the commonality of the work done by marketing. In many cases industrial marketing will become a one-to-one process; I have already discussed one-Client, advertising microagencies, for example. There will be massive product proliferation as information networking reveals to other teams within the company the products of the intensified development work. This will, in turn, shorten product life cycles even further than they have already become under the influence of modern technology.

These three factors alone promote a fascinating insight into the changes that will eventually come to marketing. They push it closer to integration with the selling role and towards an inevitable conclusion that marketing could become a very diverse process indeed; almost an individual, Customer-by-Customer process for many practitioners. Its primary information source would come from networking with other marketers in the same corporation or syndicate, with perhaps only a modest central resource for strategic counsel and training.

Total quality marketing needs total communications management

From the way the signs are pointed, and from the ideas we've been considering, it is quite clear that the existing communications management and control systems are hopelessly outdated, unsatisfactory and inadequate relics of the past. Total communications management is a philosophical concept which suggests that you must organise your communications to reflect and honour the integrity of the closer relationships that are created with Clients. Otherwise we create a magnificent five-star hotel with only one telephone line.

It was suggested earlier that the way you manage your communications presents a shaft of truth to the Customer about how individual and personal your service is. Every modern consumer has experienced this letdown, the moment when one human response to his situation has given him hope of satisfaction – and the next mass-produced missive shatters what seemed like a solution but is now revealed as an illusion.

Dear God, please send a new idea

I have researched this whole area with masses of help, advice, and discussion for nearly three years, and it seems that none of the conventional solutions fit. So the big problem with our third generation (which is a pseudonym for the future of our business!) is that it's a renegade. To solve the problem, we need some new thinking.

The thesis of total communications management is simple: in order to ensure the integrity of Customer communications within the relationship (and to overcome the communications traffic jam), one person must be given control. For classical sales and marketing structures, this is as impossible as it is impractical. Therefore, in order to ensure responsive decision-making and corporate flexibility, the responsibility must be devolved to the front end where the interaction is happening. Thus, the granular marketing force, as I have called it, is born. It operates under the mind, body and soul regime. Its creed is profitable partnership. Its operating methods are creative, committed and entrepreneurial. Its objective is to expose its brains.

Adopting the granular marketing culture recognises that:

● Buying decisions will involve more specialists. It equips each granule (Client-service group) with as many specialists as demanded by the Client relationships or niches for which they have responsibility.

- In the future we will see many more trading partnerships in which it is recognised that specialist know-how requires in-depth, intimate work from people who understand the larger issues – and therefore where their mutual development path will lead. Such relationships rely heavily on a build-up of mutual experience and are optimised by stability and longevity.

- We will see greater rationalisation of brand/product/service lines. This must happen, as we have seen, to enable the customisation that the market will require and the individual treatment and recognition it seeks. Just as direct marketers have given us a unique computer number to identify us and stop duplication, so we will have a unique person to identify and manage the relationship. For that relationship to succeed at maximum effectiveness, we must be able to seem like a small personal business, acting almost as if we had only the one Customer we are dealing with at any one time. With granular marketing structures such idealistic levels are possible, but it requires that instead of sales or marketing teams we create small autonomous business units. We are dealing here with a switch from the ability to sell to the ability to cultivate business.

Figure 19.2 illustrates a typical granule; the segment tones and patterns represent different disciplines. For example, one might have sales/marketing, product development, administration and finance. The nucleus in the centre of each group is the leader who takes overall responsibility for the team's quality, effectiveness and achievements. The segments can represent numbers of people or proportions of specialist resources. When deployed, the picture looks like this:

1. In the forward direction towards the Client, *two* styles of relationship will be cultivated, interpersonal and intergroup.

2. The exchanges take place via the matched specialists within the marketer and commissioner groups.

3. The operation, management, analysis and success of each granule is highly database dependent. Its forward (Client side external) and backward (corporate side internal and external)

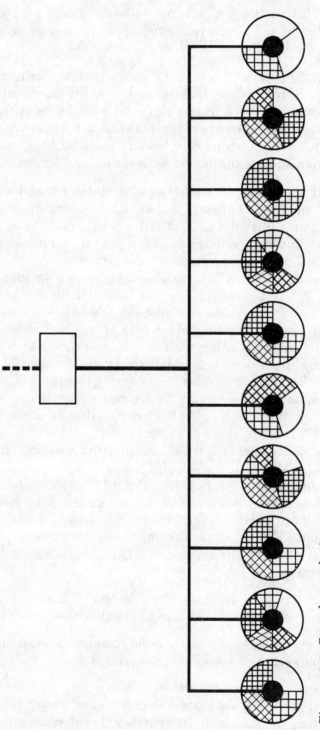

Figure 19.2: Granular marketing

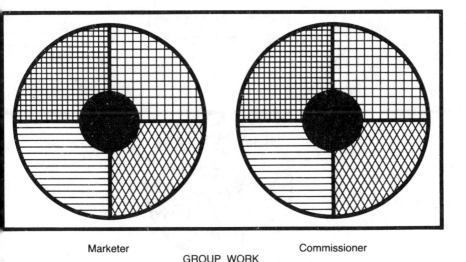

Marketer   Commissioner
GROUP WORK

Figure 19.3: The marketer and commissioner groups, a total of three teams
– two granules and the whole group together

communications requirements are fourfold in nature. You can
see that they fall into four categories:
a) *information* – to provoke inspiration;
b) *demands* – to meet the needs of the relationship;
c) *requests* – to meet the desires of the relationship;
d) *responses* – to satisfy the categories above.

4. The resources of the granule are supported and augmented by
   two banks. One is the know-how bank, which supplies
   internal and external specialists, and the other is the infobank
   – the home of the database.

5. This is a triangle and like any triangular structure will
   collapse without any one of the three, interdependent facets.
   But the most important part is the banking process – indeed,
   why it is so-called – is that it is two-way. Thus, it achieves its
   ultimate power and strength if the withdrawals do not exceed
   the deposits!

There remain three major issues in relation to decisions about new
sales and marketing structures: are these units sales and marketing
units or complete microbusinesses; how do they relate to each
other and to the corporation; and how are the personnel motivated
and rewarded?

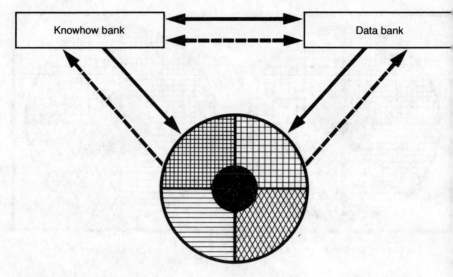

Figure 19.4: The granular marketing banking process

Microbusinesses or sales and marketing only?

As we have considered, the true product of the future for so many marketers is know-how. They will be selling to the head, an intellectual exercise. This will be true, even where, by the classical definition, the product is a manufactured item. I anticipate that where the marketing exercise has a product that is manufactured, granules will be primarily sales and marketing, although, depending on the nature of the product in question, they should be structured fully to meet all the needs of the Client which necessitate liaison and exchange. However, where there is no such production base – as in services and the professions – there are only exceptional cases where these units could not be complete microbusinesses operating with maximum power and responsiveness for their Customers' benefit. These units will effectively combine the best of a small business with the best of a large one. These two methods will look as follows:

The broadside array in Figure 19.5 has a line tie to the business centre, thus providing a pure sales and marketing extension. Effectively, sales and marketing will operate here, almost as if they were a sales and marketing company within a group, even though they are actually not truly so autonomous. In the network array (Fig. 19.6), an umbilical cord exists to the core business. This cord

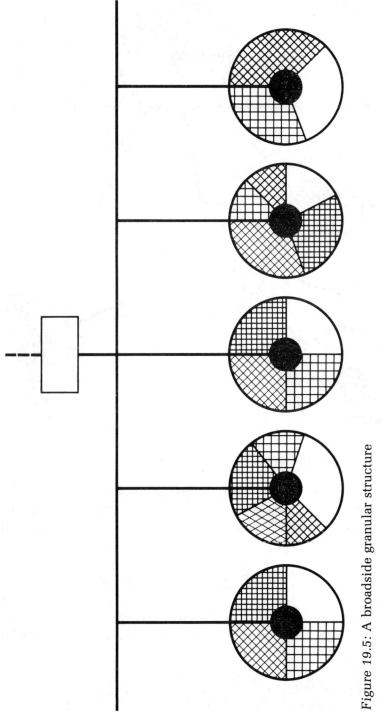

Figure 19.5: A broadside granular structure

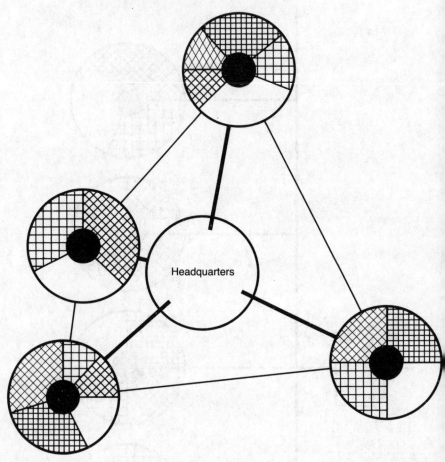

Figure 19.6: A network granular structure

carries the banking details and the performance review, goal setting and other central activities. Granules are networked to each other to maintain a leading-edge exchange of thinking and know-how.

What have we achieved?

Let us review what we have achieved by creating such structural changes. Apart from providing the means for optimum relationship building, we can see that:

1. *The old way:*
   a) encourages individual effort;

    b) discourages consultation and teamwork;

    c) promotes directionally wrong and old-fashioned values.

2. *The new way*:

    a) sponsors team effort;

    b) encourages group activity;

    c) provides the forwarding of the total corporate promise;

    d) propagates relationship values;

    e) seeks not to listen, but to understand the Client/partner.

Just as the 1980s saw the creation of centres of excellence, in the 1990s marketers will create centres of empathy.

This chapter has dealt with some matters of structure and suggested some new ideas for you to consider. They may not all relate to your business; some may relate only to those you buy from, rather than those you sell to, and therefore help them better to meet your needs. Let me endeavour to summarise the major points:

- Total quality marketing is not new. However, the structures and methods previously used are now inadequate and inappropriate. New ideas must be found.

- The idea of increasing the intensity of the classic Customer-service unit will continue to operate, for those business methods do not change. However, again, this solution is inappropriate for fostering relationships of the depth and breadth we will see in future.

- Teams are the perfect unit concept; however, marketing will need a new environment in which to flex its muscles. It will demonstrate a new maturity which is more business orientated generally and more responsible specifically.

- The rate of product development which results from customisation will create a rate of progress that will compound the innovation rate technology has already created. This has three side effects:

    1. Decisions will involve more specialists.

    2. Trading partnerships will add intimacy and stability.

    3. Rationalisation of brand/product/service lines assists customisation.

- Whether granules operate as almost wholly autonomous businesses or only as sales and marketing units will depend on whether the business has product or not. Manufacturing or product businesses may choose sales and marketing units but with vastly increased freedom and authority.

Part Four: Methods to Make Changes

20

Change – Who Needs It?

Not too many of us like change very much. And in business, coping with change is a highly specialised task. So at this point I have turned to the best specialist I know, simply the most talented management consultant with whom I have had the pleasure of working. His name is Pip Mosscrop, and he is managing director of Collinson Grant Consultants Ltd, who operate from Manchester, England.

Pip is not a writer (he tells me), so the way this section of the book works is that we have discussed the issues together. I have then written up the results which Pip and I have discussed and edited; this is just as well for Pip, since the chosen writing style at Collinson Grant is somewhat different from my own ... and might therefore give him a few awkward problems back at base!

I would, more seriously, like to record here my thanks to Pip Mosscrop and Collinson Grant for the time, expertise and information so kindly and freely given. It seemed hardly possible that, having set out by such extraordinarily different routes, we should find ourselves in the same place. It is quite uncanny and, I suspect, not a little comforting for us both.

Changemasters

Change in itself represents a challenge to business. And we have already considered the notion that more radical and increasingly relentless changes are actually happening to businesses large and small. I have also demonstrated that classic corporate structures and hierarchies, whether throughout the company or just in relation to the marketing department, can create a lack of flexibility and versatility in sales and marketing situations which could seriously hamper or retard the alacrity with which marketers will have to operate in the future. This remains true whether one is thinking of maximising the prospecting and conquest-geared activity or responding to the precise needs of Customers and seeking to protect the company from damaged or deteriorating relationships and thereby potential loss of custom.

Yet human nature, not good with change in the first place, seems to find magnification and amplification inside the booming chambers of big institutions and corporations. And, occasionally, the boardroom booms loudest and longest against change, tradition and precedent being more comfortable, less risky to deal with. Thus, as we learn more and more about an age that requires flexibility of planning as well as flexibility of thinking and attitude, attention must surely focus on the boardroom for the signal to address the future, consider new thinking and find new solutions. Leadership and direction, of which the boardroom is and will remain both the sanctuary and centre, have never been in a brighter spotlight than at this time.

Steps to changes

When you are considering changes, the following ideas will help you to judge and shape the task ahead of you.

Step 1. Know where you are

First you must carry out a review or audit of where you are and where you stand. It may be necessary or helpful to seek outside help with this since impartial judgement and unimpaired observation are keys to a successful appraisal.

Step 2. Know where you are going

Consider your ultimate goal. At this stage don't compromise this vision by letting history and experience cloud what can and can't be achieved.

Step 3. Study the gap

The gap between Step 1 and Step 2 is the task at hand. Thus, you can look at the gap as a corporate project and start to think about the methods and means.

Step 4. Identify the phasing

Most projects of this nature fall or can be divided into phases with a natural feel or rhythm to them. Just in the same way as to cross a stream you might first put down stepping stones one pace apart, recheck the positioning again from the other side once it has been reached, and then fill in or bridge the gaps to provide the completed solution.

Step 5. Create a vehicle for change

Just as, in the preceding analogy, our bridge becomes a means through (or rather over) which one can get to the other side, so we must create a corporate vehicle or process through which we can get from where we are to where we want to be.

Such vehicles might be created from training programmes, changes in management style, corporate or departmental structures, new procedures and changes to job specifications. These are the concrete mechanisms which will provide our stepping stones. Gradually, as people get a clear view of the other side – where they are going – they will, if the mechanisms are right, look forward to and feel confident about the journey.

How to find out where you are

The obvious place to start with such an examination is the Customer. However, I strongly suggest that in many situations you find a way past the 'professional' buyer if such exists in your sector. It is the specifiers and highest level thinkers whose assessment will be of most benefit to you. If you have strong ideas of where you are, or if your own sales and marketing teams have developed systems to tell them, or if you rely on the likes of Nielsen figures, checking with Customers can help you to validate theories, to discover the truth behind statistics.

Bypassing buyers may not sound very respectful of their role; however, many corporations use the buyer as a protective ring or filter. I asked earlier how people feel about quantity-driven sales-people – here is the answer! They build a defence structure to protect themselves. Quality marketing will cut through this costly, negative and wasteful charade like the brightest, sharpest knife, leaving people to build teams which move them forward faster together, rather than having one side dig a moat while the other lays seige.

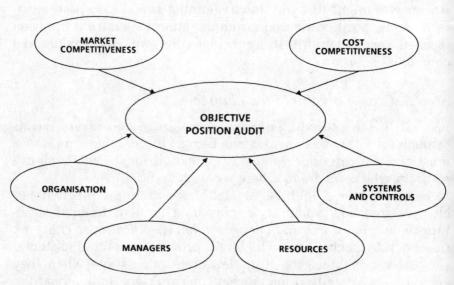

Figure 20.1: The model of objective position auditing

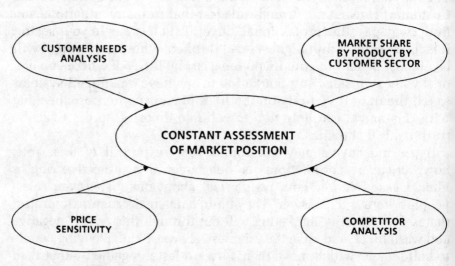

Figure 20.2: The model of constant assessment of market position

So you have the choice of building confidence with the buyer to let you through or, alternatively, finding some way of approaching those you need to reach which does not cause damage. In the final resort, the CEO-to-CEO approach here has rarely failed since, in the greater order of things, both executives recognise the potential when it is genuinely there and the approach is justified.

Assessing the gap

In assessing the task at hand or, if you will, examining the gap and looking at it as the project, it is vital to break it down into manageable segments – I'm probably not the first to describe these 'bite-size chunks'. If the process lacks natural breaks, six-month periods represent good psychological units; enough to make tangible progress; not so much that one could be expected to change the world.

It is at this time that you will need to consider and create the shape of the vehicle or process which will be used to get you across the gap. There are some imperatives to assist with this:

Identify the right issues

In auditing where you are, it is critical that you identify the right issues; that is to say, that your audit can be related accurately to the task ahead. These are likely to include the product or service, Customer support, market research, and Customer and non-Customer attitudes.

Seek third-party help

History holds examples of plenty of those who have tried to complete their task themselves and found that the one setback to self-assessment is that without checks or controls it can become self-fulfilling.

Understand the need to train and to develop experience

By far the most effective balance here will include an element of 'classroom training' and learning 'on the job', which is now more commonly regarded as a kind of counselling process.

Head for a self-measurement regime

In this context it is a clear objective in new style businesses that everyone becomes an accountant and a marketer; that is to say, that they understand the financial dynamics of their success or failure, or over- or under-performance, as well as the relationship it has with marketing. Thus, for example, salespersons will be expected to understand how price negotiations affect margin, profitability, their budget, and their pay, as well as how they affect the company's position with the Client in the long and short term. Moreover, they'll need to consider how the *way* price is negotiated will affect the company's positioning in the buyer's mind.

To operate a satisfactory self-measurement regime, the standards must be absolutely clear; the effects of success or failure must be both powerful and direct; and, wherever possible, the reward system should be automatic. Self-measurement requires that people can relate their effort to the critical part of the project (the bite-size chunk) that is in hand. A degree of classical subjective assessment will complement such regimes, since it is quite likely that, as a part of installing the quality objectives, several less tangible, qualitative and philosophical or cultural objectives will be placed upon people. We shall see more of this in Chapter 22 where we look at rewards. In effect, a self-measurement regime will play a major part in measuring the progress of change continuously and visibly.

Be open about goals, methods and achievements

There is a great deal to be said for openness in the whole matter of managing change. It tends to focus the minds of those who have chosen to come along with you. It breeds involvement, commitment and a sense of purpose. By breaking down the project into manageable tasks and applying self-measurement mechanisms to progress, the satisfaction and rewards are more readily obtained and the spoils shared. Success should yield generous rewards, and failure must be firmly acted upon.

It is true of change generally that people tend to polarise, for or against. If they don't, you should encourage them to. For, if they are not on your side, they must count as against; if they are against, then they must be helped to move on or to be found new tasks elsewhere.

It is a fact that in all elements of change there are generally casualties; people who don't fit, don't approve, or are not suitable on 'the other side', that is, when the gap has been crossed and you now occupy your new position – where you wanted to be. Generally, the more senior the dissidents, the more damage they can do. Managing change as a process is much better dealt with 'top down' and requires, or rather works most effectively, with the full support, energy, enthusiasm and commitment of all involved who want to be. And without those who don't!

Seven key factors in managing change

1. New lamps for old

Do everything you can to breed insecurity and dissatisfaction with, and distrust of, the old (present) system. Flood the people involved with evidence and reasons for change. Create and stimulate excitement, enthusiasm and interest in the new system or process.

2. Grease the chute

Changemakers need lubricants – people or media who will openly and not so openly spread the new gospel, support views, and become disciples of the project. Seek out the evangelists and give them plenty to evangelise about. Often you will find teams are an effective way of coping with change: find your best evangelists and make them prominent or even leaders in the teams. These build to a critical mass, and there comes a point where those resistant to change become 'in the wrong' as well as in the minority.

In the same way, changemakers need to seek out the healthy sections and build around them. Be fearless and surgical in dealing with the others. View them as lost causes; they are as potentially lethal as corporate cancers.

Winning the minds of those with authority, influence, desire or the freedom to change is a great facilitator and can speed change no end. And, remember, you need full commitment right from the top.

3. Sell shares and go fishing

The more people who can claim 'ownership' of the scheme or project, the greater the dedication, commitment and involvement you will generate. The earlier this can be done the wider your net can spread. Harvest as many as you can and do all you can to help them deal with problems and overcome resistance.

4. Choose your costume

Which style will your change take – will you come across as the masked avenger, the pioneering spirit, the mad scientist, the brave foot soldier or the charismatic father of change? I found the work of Harrison and Theaker both interesting and amusing when, in 1989, *Dealing with Conflict* was published. They identified the four major styles as follows:

'*Blitzkrieg / Charge of the Light Brigade Method*
Oblivious to previous history ... Personal practices, interests and antagonisms are ignored ... Fears are ridiculed ... Conflict is bloody! ... Tempers frayed! ... Tears are shed! ... Innovation fails ... Prospects of other initiatives are sabotaged! (May be used as a ploy to introduce other initiatives.)

Borgia Method
Intrigue and plots abound ... Find out potential 'blockers' ... Divide and rule ... Work out ways of 'rubbishing' their views ... Key decisions taken when they are absent from meetings ... Papers only reach them at the last minute ... Rumours are circulated about their personal habits, competence, etc. ... Any mistakes are emphasised.
(May be used as a short-term strategy.)

Munich Method
Appeasement rules OK ... Everyone must be 'nice' to one another ... Avoid 'crunch' issues ... Keep to the peripheral details ... Everyone must agree ... Therefore minimal change ...
(Everyone happy but no real development.)

Matterhorn Method
All staff involved collaboratively ... Conflict is necessary but needs to be controlled ... Stress on benefits for the group ... Team is greater than the sum of the members ... Cult of the personality is avoided ... Each member must have an opportunity to make a contribution and therefore have ownership ...
(May not always work ... if it fails ... all the team fails.)'

5. *Erect your scaffolding*

Scaffolding – or support systems – of two distinct types is required for change to proceed most smoothly. The first is personal scaffolding. This provides the means for people to deal with their personal feelings and anxieties. Change is nearly always emotive and never more so than when jobs, territories, futures and securities are involved. And that's nearly always. The second type of scaffolding is organisational, and it must:

● avoid conspiracies by providing and widely distributing accurate information;

● mould or reinforce positive ideas, actions and attitudes;

● encourage, provide and respond to feedback;

● give help, training, advice and counsel.

6. *Send in reinforcements*

Successes – however small or apparently trivial – are successes none the less and should be made much of. Publicise them as far afield as possible. They all contribute to the 'winning team' concept and will further the spirit of compliance and co-operation. This may require special (to the project) horizontal and vertical communications – and may recognise both the formal and informal (grapevines!).

Visibly identify and reward the individual and team activities or actions which, on either an individual or a team basis, support or further the change.

7. *Become a pilot*

Inside the cockpit of change you'll need to place instruments that measure the change, monitor your success and warn of deviations. You know your starting point and you know where you are headed, so you've plotted the course. However, as pilot, you need to be able to observe, calculate and make adjustments and amendments in order to achieve, not necessarily the smoothest flight, but certainly the most effective.

In this chapter, in relation to change, we have noted that:

- Planning and measuring change benefits from six key points:

  1. Know where you are.

  2. Identify, specify and agree the critical project stages.

  3. Communicate openly to gain understanding and commitment.

  4. Identify and implement managerial controls to measure performance.

  5. Reward achievement generously.

  6. Act firmly on failure.

- The strategy of change has seven steps:

  1. Analyse past trends.

  2. Evaluate objectively the current position.

  3. Identify the ultimate goal.

  4. Break the task (gap) down into manageable critical steps.

  5. Determine and agree how each of these will be tactically achieved.

  6. Plan and manage the change.

  7. Measure progress continuously and openly.

- The factors in managing change were explained and summarised as follows:

  1. Rubbish the old; worship the new.

  2. Look for people and opportunities to lubricate positive opinion.

  3. Encourage others to become co-owners of the change.

  4. Decide the style of the change.

  5. Build personal and organisational support systems.

  6. Publicise success and team or individual achievement.

  7. Monitor, measure and control the change to adopt and adjust for the best results.

21

Restructuring for Relationships

This chapter and the following deal with two of the most difficult aspects of total quality marketing. For, in assessing what comes next for sales, advertising and marketing, there are still two critical factors – the structure of the business in relation to Customer needs and the motivation of the people it employs. These matters are difficult for most organisations because they do not consider or face this kind of change every day. Indeed, most companies, let alone their marketing departments, would justifiably be lacking in this respect; specialist expertise and experience in such matters are, understandably low. Hence most companies would be well advised to consider getting outside help and advice from consultants who are able to bring both the necessary experience and expertise to support the required project and the vital objectivity of a third party.

The first piece of advice in matters of such importance and proportion as structure and rewards might follow that given in the last chapter; for even these projects can be broken down into bite-size chunks, and can be achieved through a strategic transition process. Let us, however, concentrate specifically for the rest of this chapter on structural matters and come to the rewards and motivation of employees in the next.

Marketing department or the whole organisation?

The very fact that we are facing this issue raises two important considerations. Firstly, we must realise – at least those who have any lingering doubts – that sales and marketing are not separate operational functions. They must at best fuse, or, where this is impossible or impractical, they must integrate. I expect that many companies, in practice, will actually cease to draw a distinction over the following years. There is so little merit in so many cases. It can already be argued that all marketing, in one guise or another, is selling; it is only a matter of time before the reverse should become true and that all selling will become marketing. At that point distinction loses reason.

The second consideration raised by the question of restructuring and which is highlighted by a need to decide between a marketing or corporate change is that this should not be a marketing department decision. It is a board decision. It has a wide impact on the business and, if the restructuring is successful, will change the whole balance of the business, adding much greater emphasis and power to marketing.

A new balance and therefore a new balance of power

At the moment, convention suggests that a business has assets which are its buildings, machinery, plant, people and expertise. With manufacturing businesses the valuation of assets is quite traditional; with service businesses this matter is more complicated since often its people are a most important factor. However, in tomorrow's businesses we see two other assets becoming significant. The problem for accountants is that these two assets are both intangible. The first is know-how and the second is the Customer relationships. In the latter area some pioneering work is being done, and I expect to see accounting conventions come to terms with this new thinking. More importantly, we need to appreciate that as we move from transaction businesses to relationship businesses, the fundamental shift of total quality marketing, we will no longer see individual sales transactions as the marketing units of currency. Focus will be shifted onto the relationships being built. They are more stable, more predictable, more reliable, but, at this time, less quantifiable to accountants. Gradually, as the power, effectiveness and therefore value of these relationships starts to outshine those of the traditional methods, this will create a shift in the balance of the perceived assets and their values to the company.

For many, a new view will develop that the market is a greater asset than the business. In other words, instead of building a business and constantly looking for markets to satisfy it, the balance will change to the view that, having the market – that is, the power – we must look for manufacturing or service opportunities to satisfy it. So these are the two extremes of view; where your company positions itself is what matters. For the future, however, we can be sure of a substantial swing towards those businesses which place quite significant value on the markets, a point which, incidentally, fits quite well the 1980s trends of looking anew at the asset value of brands. Indeed, if you observe how investment decisions have been magnified since the notion that brands have quantifiable asset values, you can imagine how the same concept applies to Customer relationships.

Will the board understand the decision it will be asked to make?

The extent of restructuring and the making of the decision by the board present, I believe, two hurdles to marketers. The first problem is to get a sufficient understanding of the new concepts through to those representing (and usually protective of) their own disciplines and territories. The impact on them is quite extensive if there is to be a corporate restructure. For, the businesses-within-businesses that result will devolve marketing to the front and will in most cases place marketing alongside the others in these teams. We are dealing with a potentially highly charged political issue! Thus, marketers who are making such a case must have a full and clear understanding of all the business issues before they go to the board.

It would be wrong to think that all the initiatives for changes such as those we are considering will come from within marketing. I suspect that in many cases marketing directors will be brought to consider such issues by their chief executive. This, I believe, will result in a much easier ride for all concerned. The problem here is more whether the total quality marketing effort is a corporate or departmental thrust; this problem identifies the second hurdle when the initiative comes from within marketing. Will the board understand the full issues? Or will it think those guys in marketing are having a brainstorm?

Back to the Customer again

What should lie behind the structural shape of a company? What is wrong with a hierarchy?

Common sense tells us that if the majority accept, as does tradition, one common shape to solve all problems, then that shape must have more to do with its suitability to the problem-solver than it does with the problem to be solved. For, if the business world consists of problems which fall into four types – rivets, screws, nuts and nails – a hammer will perform a task, but it will be much more effective in certain identifiable cases. Those who argue for the hammer, in favour of hierarchies, will suggest that the well-being of the problem-solver is important, since no good at all will come of a broken hammer. Those who favour autonomous business units, while agreeing that having all four of the necessary tools requires more skills, accept that the end result is vastly better, since you find the right solution to the right problem.

Total quality marketing places the Customer first – even in this decision. For, I believe, the structure of the business should facilitate its primary function. The primary function of the business is to respond to Customer needs. The optimum way to achieve this is through flexible, agile, high-energy, responsible teams. Further, to stay flexible to Customers and markets, the structures that are developed should themselves be under constant review. Is it necessary, for example, to require more of a structure than a three-year horizon? If it is, then fair enough; but convention suggests for no valid reason at all that a corporate structure should last decades.

What do Customers want of us? How do they use our products or services? What will they need next from us? These are the real issues for deciding a corporate structure. Find the answers and the board will find its structural answers.

Elegance of form

There is one further idea which you might like to think about when looking at business structures. Draw them on paper, and see how they look. For me, one of the great plus points of the hierarchy was that it had elegance of form. When the elegance was there it usually worked well. When managers had distorted the hierarchy into a shape lacking elegance, just as it looked clumsy, so was its performance.

I am not suggesting that an effective organisational structure always looks good on paper or, even more ridiculously, that if it doesn't work on paper, it won't work in fact. I do propose that structures that look right are more likely to work right, hierarchies or otherwise.

Aspects of structure

Structures have impact throughout the business. There isn't anyone who will remain unscathed or unaffected, but those to whom restructuring should make the most difference are Customers. It must also be said that flatter corporate structures make management and control both harder and more critical. The favoured posture in relation to controls is that they should be 'tight/loose'.

A business operating to 'tight/loose' controls requires that its managers should have crystal-clear objectives for which they must work and against which their performance will be tightly measured and recorded. However, the ways that they may set about achieving them will be subject to very loose controls, allowing them great freedom and responsibility.

Whatever the controls employed, other aspects of moving away from hierarchies are important. Indeed, you can expect to lose some valuable benefits for which you must be careful to make provision in a new structure. For example, how do you harness corporate pride? How do you build corporate commitment? Both these important requirements must be engendered for an effective business that has confidence in its ability and belief in its standards.

Within the hierarchy these qualities tend to breed quite well, since both the system and the culture enjoy and often reward them, but this is not the case with fragmented structures or autonomous business units. With these you have to take positive steps to encourage them and help them grow. This is achieved through the provision of procedures, processes and communications media. It is important that these units do not become too wrapped up in themselves and therefore place all their allegiance and commitment within their own teams. They must not lose sight of the fact that they are part of the greater structure and must maintain high key attitudes to corporate desires and strategies.

To some extent, this can be underlined by performance and pay, but information systems and communications will also be of great benefit. This moves information and communications systems to centre stage. With regard to those, the following are the key issues:

● *Flat structures do not need elaborate committee networks*, but they do need a free flow of information and ready access.

- A conference technique can be used to integrate management. This has three benefits:
  - It provides clarity of purpose.
  - It reinforces motivation.
  - It subjects executives to 'trial by peers'.

The conference technique pulls together the key managers of the organisation once a year. They will typically spend a highly charged and highly taxing week together, tackling the next year's plan and budget. Basically, no one escapes until both are agreed. Operating rather like a prime minister's cabinet (but probably with much greater effectiveness!), the team have to face all the issues of that business, fight all their departmental battles, agree the corporate priorities, and assent to the corporate objectives. There is no doubt this is a gruelling process, but it is being used more and more to great effect.

- *Leadership development is by exposure rather than by training alone* – we realised earlier that these flatter organisational structures, as the levels are reduced, take from the organisation a training ground that has for centuries proved highly effective and extremely cost-effective. Thus, provision must be made to put back this vital resource. In terms of day-to-day training, a resource can be created for 'classroom' training which will augment on-the-job learning. However, leaders need to be identified and brought forward. Businesses have found – as, incidentally, have many educationalists – that leaders need to be given a chance to shine; that given the freedom to operate, leaders often lift themselves above the crowd; and that the tougher the targets or tasks they are given, the greater the qualities and the ingenuity they display.

  If your system doesn't give such people a chance to stick their heads over the parapet and be noticed, then you'll never know they are there. Often systems, procedures or traditions mask our potential leaders from us and leave them frustrated in an inhibitive regime where everybody is average – and, sadly, this becomes the accepted level. Leaders often may not be good at one or two of the steps convention says they must take. Or, one hardly dares to suggest it, perhaps they should actually skip a level! It's really about bringing out the best in your people and being sure that the system cultivates leaders rather than squashing them.

- *Operational communications follow the line of the profit chain,* meaning that instead of being organised by function, as they are at the moment in hierarchies, communications are reorganised to follow a direct process pattern, eg Customer – marketer – product/service. At the moment, quite complex chains of approval or agreement can be required to gain, say, approval for some special arrangement for a Customer. In order to obey the chain of command, a salesperson wishing to approach a production person will route his request via his manager to the production manager and down to the production person. When the chain permits or even encourages direct communication it is far more responsive to Customer need. Of course, if the autonomous business unit structure is adopted, the perfect solution prevails, since production is represented within the unit.

Handling information systems

The information systems of the new structure will be critical and information systems have some characteristics that should be recorded here. It's likely you'll already have suffered from these in some way, but let's recall them anyway:

- Computer systems are helpful but not essential. This sounds obvious. Indeed it is. But most people still place an expectation on the computer system which is preposterous and unachievable. Computer systems may be helpful – a universal remedy they are not!

- Managers always seriously underestimate the preparation time required to implement the systems, the resources that will be needed, and the costly, time-wasting, frustrating disruption that is created.

- Software is always late. Always!

- Inadequate thought and effort always go into the disciplines which should ensure data integrity and accuracy. This is always discovered too late and costs too much to correct, and accurate systems take too long to become operational.

Broadside or network?

The final consideration of this chapter is whether you should deploy your new sales and marketing or business units in a 'broadside array' or as a 'networked structure'. The answer will depend entirely on the decision you considered at the beginning of this chapter. Are you planning to adopt sales and marketing units or autonomous business units? If sales and marketing, go broadside; if autonomous business units, because of their self-sufficiency, go network. All this is just as we discussed at the end of Chapter 19.

To summarise, this chapter presented the following ideas:

- Businesses do not have to deal on a day-to-day basis with such matters as changes to infrastructure and pay and reward systems. Therefore, it is unlikely that sufficient specialist skills about such sensitive and critical issues will be found in-house. External consultants or advisers can provide a cost-effective and more experienced way to see the project through.

- The distinction between sales and marketing is about to disappear. We should assist this.

- The issue of reshaping to get closer to Customers is an issue which reaches to the heart of the organisation; as such, it is a board issue, not a departmental issue.

- The notion that Customer relationships have an asset value will change the power balance of companies and enhance the role and value of marketing.

- Marketing has a dual hurdle in presenting its case to the board: firstly, it must make the directors aware of all the issues; secondly, it must make them understand the deep and critical significance of this matter. In other words, this is a corporate survival matter.

- Corporate structures should be elegant in design and must reflect the needs of the Customer. However, it is foolish to think of this in a rigid way: for, in future, structures will become more flexible and more responsive to Customer needs.

- Flatter structures benefit from 'tight/loose' management controls which give clear objectives and firm measurement but great freedom of action and decision-making.

- Some benefits get lost when hierarchies are flattened out. It is therefore important that specific provision be made for them. Vehicles must be found to harness corporate pride and foster corporate commitment.

- With regard to information systems, the following factors should be remembered:

    1. Elaborate committee networks are not required.

    2. A conference technique can be used to integrate management effectively. This provides clarity of purpose, reinforces motivation and subjects executives to trial by peers.

- Leadership development is by exposure as well as training. The whole process of 'growing' people is different outside hierarchies. We must give potential leaders the opportunity to shine; otherwise, they may simply be absorbed into the mass. Good people respond to tough targets and assignments, reaching heights they themselves may not have realised they could achieve.

- Operational communications should follow the profit chain, not the business disciplines, and should be free of social and political precedents.

- With regard to the planning and implementation of new information systems, these factors are common:

    1. Systems are helpful but are not a universal remedy.

    2. No computer systems are easy to get in, up and running.

    3. Time, resources, disruption and costs are always underestimated.

    4. Software is always late.

    5. Data-accuracy disciplines are never good enough.

- If total quality marketing ideas for relationship building are to be implemented on a departmental basis, a broadside array is recommended; if on a corporate basis, a network structure.

22

Refocusing Rewards

Total quality marketing requires an enormous leap in the mentality of sales, advertising and marketing people. Indeed, I would suggest that even those who do not feel it appropriate to follow, for example, the advice of the last chapter will, nevertheless, find it necessary to change or modify their reward systems. The primary purpose must now be to encourage and reward success; the secondary, where restructuring has taken place, will be to put back the other elements that have disappeared. Remember that when hierarchies are abandoned for the new flatter structure, one element of the reward system has been effectively removed – promotion. The demise of the middle manager casts a long shadow!

So, there can be no better time to step back from the task at hand and consider the role of pay and reward systems, both as a motivational tool and for nurture and propagation of our quality goals.

Rewards – how they relate to the corporate mission

When projects like reorganisation or cultural shift are under way, the spirit to drive this through will come essentially from three sources. These are the reservoir of corporate pride, a sense of sacrifice in the common good and, of course, powerful incentives for excellent performance. Such incentives tend to work best when the schemes are simple and cover all employees. Typically, these are geared to different factors, depending on the level of employee. For example:

Shop floor	– productivity based
Staff	– related to productivity or cost control; meeting Customer and quality requirements
Management	– performance against unit costs and/or margins
Executives	– performance versus return on capital employed
	– share options
	– Customer satisfaction and loyalty

It is vital that pay must follow the culture or mission, not lead it, thereby, in effect, reinforcing objectives, not driving them; that it push rather than pull.

The politics of remuneration

When you lift the roof of any company, rather like a community of ants or bees, you can observe a society at work. The society, in matters such as remuneration, sets the tone of what are acceptable and unacceptable norms. As so often in life, pecking orders are established, and so comparisons will be drawn. You might find this to be in relation to capability – skilled to unskilled; in relation to professional training – accountants to engineers; and in relation to geography – the South East to the rest of the UK. As you move up and down the pecking orders, you see the balance between cash and fringe benefits change. Then, you will observe a reward factor which is the use of profit as a motivator.

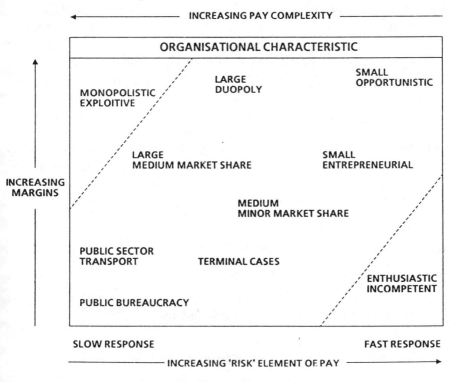

Figure 22.1: The remuneration map: different organisational styles have different remuneration systems

Next you will notice that the society or community establishes dynamics which influence the style and level of pay. This is illustrated by my remuneration map (Fig. 22.1). You will see how typical, fast-growing companies have high-risk elements, while mature companies place greater emphasis on benefits, and bureaucracies have elaborate, defensive systems.

Deciding the objectives of pay reform

To go with the implementation of total quality marketing, we have identified two pivotal roles for our pay and reward system: we want it to assist with the restructuring in some cases, but in all cases we want it to play a long-term and significant part in the transfer from quantity to quality objectives.

One simple example will illustrate how this latter point is effected. Consider the change which occurs for a salesperson who is moved from commission on short-term sales to commission on long-term profits. All of a sudden the salesperson modifies his whole negotiating stance, finding new ways to lure Customers. Plainly, this shows that we can achieve our objectives and underpin our corporate changes of direction. However, we need to think how our people, not just the salespeople, but all appropriate people, can be made to concentrate on relationship building.

Before looking at the factors which we can use, perhaps we should consider whether there are any other objectives which should also influence our thinking. As well, of course, as its motivational impact in enhancing corporate pride or commitment and recognising business, marketing or sales performance, pay reform can also recognise:

- cost control or reduction;

- the attraction or retention of key staff;

- changing employee behaviour.

Of one thing you can be certain, it is the business need which will dictate the direction of change and that means ...

... Back to Customers, once again

Since the driving force in our decision-making is now the Customer relationship, we can broaden the scope to consider what I call 'geared motivation'. This has three major aspects. Firstly, it rewards business growth, not simply sales. Secondly, it brackets rewards. And, thirdly, it offers a range of 'gearing factors', which include more qualitative factors than quantitative.

The concept of bracketing rewards is fundamental to the quality mission. By setting minimum levels below which little, preferably no, reward is triggered, one effectively sets a minimum acceptable performance standard or average. By setting maximum levels, one inhibits overemphasis on aspects which might detract from the declared goals. This clearly could dissuade those who place too much value on the sales element and enourage them to focus on other aspects of their work. For example, a salesperson who is paid 10 per cent commission up to 80 per cent of target, 12 per cent up to 100 per cent of target, and 15 per cent thereafter is basically going to screw every last sale out of anyone that steps in his path.

Thus, equally, it can be appreciated that, just as by putting a minimum bracket the minimum standards are laid down, so by putting a maximum ceiling for reward it is clearly demonstrated that selling to win more commission and to fulfil personal goals is not what is required. What is added now are the qualitative gearing factors. Let us take a look at what I mean by gearing factors:

- sales;
- profitability;
- spread of business;
- longevity of relationship;
- Customer satisfaction;
- problem-free periods;
- research results;
- initiative;
- innovation;
- team spirit/activity;
- personal spirit/activity.

Of course, you can add more to these – to suit whatever your corporate desires are. Your selection of factors becomes the criteria against which employees are measured. However, none of them need necessarily relate directly to sales or turnover (not even the sales factor); they could all relate to corporate performance, however you choose to measure that.

To be clear about the possibility that the sales factor might not be related to sales, let's take an example since the explanation of gearing factors is confusing when you write about it, let alone when you read it! You may choose to give a salesperson a salary which, on target, is set to provide, say 80 per cent basic and 20 per cent from rewards. Of the 20 per cent rewards, you have chosen your gearing factors so that actual sales turnover generated will provide 25 per cent of that, ie 5 per cent of total pay. However, the 'pot' from which the rewards are paid does not have to be a sales-generated pot. It can be generated by items which are much more closely related to corporate success. Such a calculation will ensure that the time investment by the salesperson is well thought out, but also that he knows that at the end of the day a happy, satisfied Customer leads to happy, satisfied employers, leading to happy, satisfied employees. I said earlier that simplicity was a good quality to strive for in a pay-and-reward system; it is, but, alas, it's not always so easy to achieve. For an example of pure courage and vision, and achievement of the notion of simplicity, read the Rank Xerox story in the next chapter.

Incidentally, when setting the pay and gearing factors, it is always easier to start from the amount you want your people to receive when they get the job right, and then work back to decide how your gearing factors will deliver that. So, if you want someone on target to earn £20,000, of which 10 per cent should be performance related, set the basic at £18,000 and then decide how you wish to deal with the rest. For ease, let's say the system will cut in at 80 per cent of target and cut out at 120 per cent. Thus, this employee will not earn less than £19,000 nor more than £21,000. Systems like this can be operated to pay the rewards monthly, quarterly or annually if you prefer. Now all you have to do is decide on what basis the reward will be allocated.

Specify the job you want done

We cannot really consider pay-and-reward systems without a word about job specifications, since the two should be locked together. When you change what you need from your staff, it is essential that the new elements be incorporated into their job specification (and, for that matter, the old removed). Each aspect should be discussed in detail with the employee and, where relevant, the correlation with the reward system clearly explained. Where subjective judgement or assessment is to be used (and that's probably in a great deal of areas), the methods of measurement and control must be abundantly clear to the individual employees. Also, they must be just as clear about new operational procedures.

When preparing the job specifications, try to remember the 'tight/loose' idea and give people more freedom to move, but in a more tightly defined direction. One way you can prove whether you have constructed these mechanisms properly is to ask each of your staff to report to you on how they would relate these changes through to each Customer. If that is not possible – because of scale – get them to nominate a number of Customers or a number of clusters of Customers and then report on their new responsibilities and tasks.

When considering the remuneration strategy for your employees, whatever their grade, it is worth remembering that four factors should be pulled together by pay: the style and culture of the business, the objectives of the business, the structures and societies in which your people work, and last, but always first in fact, what your Customers want and need of you.

Changing systems of remuneration

It is needless to remind you, I'm sure, but pay is a sensitive and emotive issue. Changes to existing systems should be planned and executed carefully. However, to assist you in that process, I have no hesitation in proposing the formula from Chapter 20. That's to say, examine where you are, decide where you want to be, and see the gap as the task. Bite-size chunks may come to your rescue again, and there is no reason whatsoever why you cannot run a transition period for, say, two or three years, achieving one or two steps towards the end result each year.

This chapter has taken a fundamental look at pay and rewards in relation to total quality marketing and described how you can think about what has to come next. In summary ...

- When structures are flattened, one of the great motivational factors for employees – promotion – is severely hindered. This focuses their minds on other aspects.

- Rewards should relate directly to the corporate mission. Simple schemes covering all employees are generally the most effective.

- Pay must follow the corporate culture or mission, not lead it. Figure 22.1 on page 219 shows a typical example demonstrating that fast-growing companies have high-risk elements, mature companies have an emphasis on benefits, and bureaucracies have elaborate defensive systems.

- The major objectives to be influenced by pay reform are:

    1. cost control or reduction;

    2. the attraction or retention of key staff;

    3. changing employee behaviour;

    4. enhancement of corporate pride and commitment;

    5. recognition of business, marketing, or sales performance.

- Motivational elements of remuneration should reflect the desires of the Customers. Geared motivation widens rewards from conventional quantity objectives:

    1. It rewards business growth.

    2. It brackets rewards.

    3. It recognises, measures and rewards quality.

- Gearing factors can include:

    1. sales;

    2. profitability;

    3. spread of business;

    4. longevity of relationship;

    5. Customer satisfaction;

    6. problem-free periods;

    7. research results;

    8. initiative;

    9. innovation;

    10. team spirit/activity;

    11. personal spirit/activity.

- Job specifications have a direct link to the pay-and-reward policy. New elements of the specification should be explained clearly to staff and the relationship to the pay system underlined where appropriate.

- Job specifications should be modified at the first opportunity to give employees as much freedom to move as possible, but in a tightly controlled direction.
- Sales and marketing employees should be able to prepare a plan (in accordance with their new specification) for each Customer. Where numbers preclude this, they should prepare a plan for a representative sample of Customers or, at the least, individual clusters or sectors of Customers.
- Remuneration systems can be changed using the steps set out in Chapter 20.

23

Well on the Way: Case Histories

It is perhaps strange that within such a short time of IBM's featuring in Tom Peters and Robert Waterman's book *In Search of Excellence* as one of the 'excellent' companies, IBM should come to its own conclusion that it had drifted away from Customers and 'taken its eye off the ball'. Some of this will have as much to do with time passing as anything which perhaps could actually be laid at the door of IBM's management, except that they lost sight of what was happening around them. Of course, I implied earlier that they should have known better; yet, it could be said in IBM's defence it was an unhappy accident that such a huge corporation should be drifting, rudderless, away from its Customers (as a result of building and perpetuating such huge and cumbersome hierarchies) at exactly that moment in history which determined that the computer industry, perhaps more than any other, needed to get so close as to be intimate with its Customers.

With a company like IBM we are dealing with a metaphorical supertanker. Yet for each hour that you might expect it to take such a large marine giant to come to a stop, turn completely about and reaccelerate in the opposite direction, such a corporate giant might take a year. I prefer to see such imperatives considered in 'bite-size chunks' regardless of the size of the business. For they will be just as vital and just as radical and just as difficult in every case. After all, whether a supertanker, tanker, trawler or wind-surfer, if it's heading towards the end of the world, oblivion waits in every case.

'Bite-size chunks' were also to be found at Rank Xerox. There, the chief executive officer at the time, Roland Magnin, had different problems and was considering very different solutions – so different they make a fascinating example of whether your declared mission, corporate culture and pay mechanism work in harmony or discord. Magnin pulled the three together and the results, although taking time to show, proved sweet music to everyone's ears.

One would perhaps imagine that a service company might have an easier task when it comes to making major corporate adjustments. In fact, this is not the case. And so the calm, controlled and considered approach taken by Royal Insurance (UK) Ltd looks set to pay huge dividends.

These three stories look at the most radical way that one starts putting the quality back into marketing and focuses the business tightly on the primary marketing objective of building relationships. I present them in the hope that they will encourage others to think about what they are doing. For each of these case histories demonstrates how powerfully just a few of the ideas within the principles expounded in this book will work for you.

The largest Customerisation in the world

When you decide to take a massive, global industry leader, shake it up, and change its whole posture, inevitably the task is as gargantuan as it is expensive as it is risky. Therefore, correctly, IBM's huge task required the commitment of everyone it employed and its shareholders.

IBM had lost sight of its Customers' needs. It had grown into a bureaucratic monolith. Decisions were slow, productivity overall poor, and Customer attitudes negative. Many IBM Customers, while appreciative of the products, felt they had been taken advantage of or even trapped into long-term dealings. Clearly, it was time for IBM to act.

By the end of 1989, IBM's annual report showed a project charge of $2,420 million ($1,500 million after tax), or $2.58 a share. What was IBM getting for its money?

Focusing on the Customer

In 1988, CEO John Akers reorganised the core company, IBM USA, into seven autonomous business units: PCs, mainframes, microcomputers, communications, microchip manufacturing, programming, and software, with an eighth unit that handles marketing for all the others.

Akers declared, 'I believe the IBM company must become the world's champion in meeting the needs of Customers,' and as a part of that process IBM realised that it had to listen to its Customers; the old exploitation selling methods were at last on their way out. In 1986 key Customers were to participate in IBM's internal strategic-planning conference. The following year (Akers designated it 'The Year of the Customer') IBM users were invited to participate during design and introductory product stages. By the time the AS400 computers were launched, almost 2000 of the machines had been tested by potential buyers.

In the following years, salespeople were instructed, 'Just say yes'. Their commission system was overturned and the number of units sold or rented removed as the reward base. IBM entered into joint ventures with software specialists and started to talk about and consider the notion of open systems. These were clear steps in support of long-term Customer satisfaction and away from short-term, opportunity-based quantity methods.

Since 1986, IBM has increased the number of people working directly with Customers by 23 per cent. This expected the population of IBM (USA) to fall by at least 10,000 during 1990. The year-end figure of 206,000 represented a reduction of 37,000 from the 1985 peak, and a return to the level of 1981. The costs of these operations was to be offset by reducing the company's ongoing cost and expense rate by approximately $1 billion per year.

IBM's strategy, outlined in 1985, was in recognition of the scope of the challenges it faced:

1. Rapid strides in technology and product innovations had brought about millions of new computer users.

2. Manufacturing efficiencies had resulted in excess capacity throughout the industry, and there were pressures on prices, margins and profitability.

3. Competition, from one-person, software-consulting firms to major global companies, was intense.

IBM aimed to become leaner, more efficient and, most importantly, market driven.

Greater efficiency

Since 1985, IBM has taken a series of actions to reduce its costs, expenses and structure, and to sharpen its competitiveness world-wide. These include:

1. consolidated manufacturing capacity;

2. operating with fewer layers of management;

3. reduced overheads and indirect positions by some 50,000, while maintaining the tradition of full employment.

Restructuring

Headquarters operations worldwide have been streamlined. To move more resources and authority closer to Customers, seven lines of business (Akers' version of autonomous business units) have been established. These organisations are responsible for developing and manufacturing product and service solutions for Customers.

The company launched the largest retraining and redeployment programme in its history, asking IBMers around the world to change jobs, careers and work habits in order to become more responsive to Customer needs. Over the past three years:

- 60,000 people were retrained and reassigned to new jobs.

- Of these, 30,000 were switched from overhead positions into sales, systems engineering, programming, etc.

- Between 1986 and 1989, one out of every five overhead jobs (about 50,000) was eliminated.

- By 1990 over half of all IBM employees are doing work directly involved with developing, making, marketing or servicing Customer solutions.

- IBM has taken significant actions to expand its marketing force, achieving a total of over 70,000 marketing people working with Customers, 23 per cent more than before. IBM continued to invest heavily in software development. By 1990, IBM's software development population grew to about 35,000 employees world-wide, approximately 59 per cent more than in 1986. Much of this growth came from the ranks of redeployed or retrained employees.

Ranking quality higher

The Rank Xerox story is an interesting example since we can see how it successfully moved quality objectives into its sales department as well as throughout the rest of the company.

There is a story about Roland Magnin which I have not been able to confirm. Thus, it might be more prudent to call it a fable. The fable is that, worried that his new salary and reward package might face a somewhat doubtful passage through the coming board meeting at which he would propose it, Magnin announced it first to the press, presenting his board with something of a *fait accompli*.

At the time, Magnin was chief executive of Rank Xerox. He was responsible for a change in focus which was to have a major impact on the performance of the company and enable the sales and marketing teams to adopt quality practices – indeed, it demanded that they did so.

It was explained earlier that the use of total quality management techniques can result in highly satisfactory performance changes within organisations chasing product, service and organisational improvements. However, it is suggested that total quality management will increase sales. It will. But harnessed to the power of total quality marketing, the results are faster and bigger. Rank Xerox realised that even if the product was excellent, there would be no improvements if the salespeople did not understand their Customers and get closer to them, or even, for that matter, if after-sales and maintenance standards did not similarly match up. The company also recognised that, whatever was done, it had to be a long-term or permanent programme. Indeed, such initiatives always tend to start slowly and gather momentum as the enthusiasm and commitment grows, lubricated by early success. However, in the last respect – success – Rank Xerox had a long while to wait. And, in the early years of the initiative the company refashioned and remodelled thinking as it moved forward. For example, profit had always been its number-one objective. Later this was changed to return on assets, but after three years of total quality management methods, Customer satisfaction became the prime business objective. After one year of experimentation, Roland Magnin reported as follows.

The first year

The scheme applied to the most senior managers in International Headquarters and the European operating companies (135 people in total).

The principles

The size of salary increases for these senior managers at the end of the year was influenced equally by Customer satisfaction and

Customer loyalty. Customer loyalty is defined as the proportion of products with Customers at the start of the year which are still with Customers at the end of the year. This is measured internally by Rank Xerox. The calculation is:

$$\frac{\text{Products with Customers at the start of the year minus losses during the year}}{\text{Products with Customers at the start of the year}}$$

Products are weighted by their price and allowance is made where Customers trade in a Rank Xerox product for another Rank Xerox product.

Customer satisfaction was measured by external agencies through a written questionnaire which asked:

'Are you satisfied with the products and services provided by Rank Xerox?'

'If you need another or a replacement product would you seriously consider Rank Xerox as a supplier?'

'If asked, would you recommend Rank Xerox to business associates?'

The answers were compared to norms established through Rank Xerox's more extensive surveys of Customer satisfaction.

The target levels for loyalty and satisfaction were each 85 per cent.

The link with salary increases

The results of the measures of Customer satisfaction and Customer loyalty determined whether senior managers received salary increases which were higher or lower than other staff in their country, with the override that the results would vary by a maximum of 4 percentage points up or down.

For example:

Country A
Loyalty and satisfaction results are 25 per cent better than target

General salary increase is planned at 10 per cent

Therefore, senior managers receive 12.5 per cent
(ie 10% + 25% of 10%)

Country B

Loyalty and satisfaction results are 10 per cent below target

General salary increase is planned at 8 per cent

Therefore, senior managers receive 7.8 per cent
(ie 8% minus 10% of 8%)

The general manager in each country has discretion to vary the increases for individual senior managers within the overall figure.

The salary rises for senior managers at international head-quarters were based on a composite of the results across Europe.

The results

The results show that 89 per cent of Rank Xerox Customers said they were satisfied – and the Customer loyalty level was 88 per cent. On average this boosted the salary increase of senior managers by an extra 2.5 per cent.

Changes for year 2

In the following year the scheme for senior managers continued with these changes:

● Greater weighting was given to Customer loyalty. This accounted for 70 per cent of the measurement, not 50 per cent.

● Customer satisfaction was measured as part of the regular, more detailed surveys and not separate questionnaires.

● The Customer satisfaction surveys measured perceptions of Rank Xerox against the main competitor in each product group in each country.

● The target levels of performance for loyalty and satisfaction were increased to 88 per cent.

Extension to others

A bonus was introduced for staff at international headquarters. This was calculated on the same basis as the salary rises. The European operating companies were asked to introduce similar schemes suited to their national environment.

As we have learned earlier in this book, the payoff was long and slow.

Long-term results report

After three years of dedication to quality and Customer satisfaction, they saw no visible improvement. In the fourth year – they saw real gains start. In the fifth year – profits were up 40 per cent, return on assets had trebled, unit costs of components had fallen by over 30 per cent and, very importantly, indices of Customer satisfaction had risen by 35 per cent. Rank Xerox were regaining some of the market share lost in the early 1980s.

The original problem at Rank Xerox had stemmed from the panic discovery that its rigging costs were about equal to the selling price of its Japanese competitors. This led to the realisation in due course, that rigging was not the disease but a symptom; Rank had a corporate problem. The results the company has achieved demonstrate that a process of leadership through quality can be highly effective, but that the effects will be boosted when quality reaches beyond the product and touches the Customer. Rank's evidence of an increasing performance linked to its Customers' satisfaction and loyalty clearly substantiates that building relationships with Customers has worked for the company and that, over time, it is more profitable.

Royal directions

Royal Insurance (UK) Ltd is a wholly owned subsidiary of Royal Insurance PLC, the parent holding company of one of the world's largest insurance groups operating in over 80 countries.

At the helm of Royal Insurance (UK) Ltd as its managing director was Peter F. Duerden. Mr Duerden was to lead the company through a sustained strategy of change; he correctly believed that a key characteristic of successful businesses is their ability to respond to changes in the marketplace before there is any widely held perception of the need to do so. Of course, there is the risk that the perception could turn out to be wrong – or even that action could be so pre-emptive as to be knocked off course by actual events. However, the 1980s proved to hold dramatic change for UK financial markets – legislation, 'the Big Bang', and other events were to create both problems and opportunities that left hardly anyone in the financial or property fields unscathed. Even Peter Duerden remarked, 'There can be few periods in the long and successful history of Royal Insurance in which the pace of change has been as dramatic and challenging.'

Royal identified the most significant changes as follows:

1. Its Clients were making increasingly sophisticated demands of the business.

2. The legislative and other changes turned up the heat in the marketplace, increasing competition.

3. The technological advances had effectively created different ways to transact the insurance business.

As a result, Royal, deciding to act from a position of strength, began a comprehensive review of its operations. It was anxious to make any changes necessary but had determined that the most important element had to be a new approach which focused more closely on its different kinds of Clients. It further recognised that such changes would not come cheap, requiring, as they undoubtedly would, substantial investment in systems technology and in training its people. Along with this recognition came the acceptance that Royal had to be more innovative in product design and servicing and more able to deal with change.

Royal reviewed Clients' needs within each of its principal channels of business; these it determined as:

● national brokers;

● financial service intermediaries;

● local brokers;

● agents.

The conclusion was that Royal had to change its organisation as well as many of its decision-making processes. Naturally, such radical changes had to be implemented step-by-step. The first step, dubbed 'Channel Focus', was to establish specialist teams dedicated to dealing with the different sources of business. Royal had realised, and was to reflect this realisation in its organisation, both at head office and the branches, that if its Clients had different expectations of the company, it was counterproductive to try to force them all into the same response, delivery and service mechanisms.

Furthermore, and showing great courage and insight in an industry not overburdened with such qualities, Royal set about devolving the decision-making authority in relation to the vast majority of its day-to-day business operations. This authority, passed down to the staff closest to its Clients – its branches – required a new structure with highly skilled insurance people at branch level.

The branches would report through an area branch, which would, therefore, have an unprecedented level of technical expertise and resources, enabling it to operate with substantial authority and virtual autonomy. With only six branches on average reporting to each area branch Royal had broken insurance industry tradition and provided the means for decision-making that was better quality and quicker too. Clients would benefit from this greatly enhanced decision-making capability, which covered:

- business development and underwriting;

- claims handling and processing;

- underwriting services, personnel and administration.

Thus, Royal Insurance had found a way to become more responsive to Clients' needs, but it also wanted to get closer to Clients. This meant two further steps had to be taken: the first to increase understanding of the Clients' needs, and the second to translate that understanding into an overall direction for the business. The action taken to increase understanding was the provision of specialist development teams placed strategically throughout the country. Each of these was assigned the task of responding to the needs of a particular Client group. Simultaneously, to influence the way the business responded to the changes demanded by its market, the head office in Liverpool was realigned into the same broad groups as identified by the channel focus.

With these new methods and structures in place, Royal recognised that it had made some adventurous and challenging decisions for its industry; it recognised that its traditional bureaucratic and hierarchical systems would be the undoing of all the potential good that had been done. With the new accent very much driven by the relationships it wished to create with its intermediary Clients, the decision-making process was further lubricated by the adoption of flatter corporate structures, as levels of management were stripped out.

Along with its reaffirmed commitment to new technology and radically enhanced claims operations, Royal became confident that it was now in the optimum position for the 1990s and capable of creating precedents and setting standards that would give its competitors a great deal to match; for, one aspect which the new Royal now brought to the tradition-bound business of insurance was its more innovative and entrepreneurial style.

Of course, these changes took some three years to complete, and they demonstrate yet again that to deliver quality to the market many changes must take place outside the true remit of marketing. In this instance time will prove whether or not marketing is able to maximise the full opportunity it has been given.

As an observer, I find two factors interesting about the Royal story. In many ways it could be classified a textbook example in changing direction: a prime case of a huge company doing its utmost to change from one of those faceless, self-perpetuating, self-obsessed monsters that manipulate markets to their own ends, to a new leaner, keener, versatile and energetic group of Client-orientated units that live and breathe Customer needs. My first point is that although these benefits will all, in time, supposedly benefit the end-user Customer – the policyholder – in all its reshaping and rethinking, Royal seems to have started in the middle – centring all changes on the intermediary Client. The assumption here is that the benefits will reach the policyholder in the end. I hope so, but benefits have a strange habit of being hijacked and recredited to others. Royal's intermediary Clients may steal a lot of its thunder. In the IBM example, although the roles of distributors and agents are recognised, the end-Customer was the driving force for change and, indeed, the person on whom it all focused.

Secondly, I find it strange that this revolution (for that is what it is in insurance terms) should have taken place in just one Royal Group company. If you are a British Customer of Royal, you may deal with Royal Insurance for your general business (such as household or motor insurance) and Royal Life for your life, savings and pension products. I suspect that, for most prospects and policyholders, the name *Royal* is the name they remember. They do not appreciate that there is a difference between Royal Life and Royal Insurance. Yet now, of course, there is a real difference. This vast cultural difference can serve only to confuse Customers who, since both companies are, after all, within the same group, may understandably expect some similarity in methods, systems and services. The more the changes at Royal Insurance become effective, the greater the problem could become; but, equally, perhaps they might persuade the rest of the group to follow its lead.

At ICI, admittedly in a totally different market, this problem has also reared its head. Managers have had to consider the total needs of some of their Customers. This often stretches beyond the conventional product disciplines which are recognised by ICI. After all, a Customer who buys fertilisers, on the one hand, and plastics for packaging, on the other, sees himself not as two separate Customers of ICI, but as one. Only ICI separates its needs, and it does so to meet ICI structures.

This has led ICI to look at Customers' total industry requirements. Yet individual companies or operating divisions within groups can often be quite competitive and jealously guard their information and contacts. Such petty insecurities may not exist within ICI, but I have often seen the most outrageous non-co-operation between group members. ICI has said that it feels the answer might lie in putting together its businesses in structures aligned to the marketplace; one structure for automotive, another for packaging, another for agriculture, and so on. From the outside this would seem to be a correct move, provided that:

● Each business group can quickly assimilate sufficient expertise in its new specialisation and convince its market of the benefits.

● Provision is made for the forwarding of the overall corporate strategy and culture.

● A network for information and communication is created between the market-aligned fragments.

One tendency with market-aligned fragments is for, as it were, an overflow of commitment to its market sector. This, in turn, leads each to see its resource demands as the highest priority. When the correct communication, training and information networks are in place, a much better balance between corporate direction and strategy and market-sector obsession is achieved. This is another area where the 'conferencing' technique referred to in Chapter 21 will be beneficial.

In this chapter we have looked at two examples of a restructuring solution to the problem of getting closer to Customers and building better relationships. In the case of Rank Xerox, quality standards were introduced to the sales and marketing processes and elsewhere in the business by taking a fresh look at the way its people were motivated through the pay and rewards packages.

Look for your own examples

In order to find case histories to which readers could relate, I have chosen three well-known names. However, there are many, many others already making such changes.

Look around you. Talk to your peers. You'll find examples too. They are not all big companies or 'household' names. Many are small, local companies who have realised that they, too, are not exempt or safe from the dangers of today's turbulent times.

Any company can enjoy the benefits of quality. Surely, the point which matters most is that quality as a management technique is a part of the solution. Quality as a marketing creed is, if anything, even more powerful. However, the two used in tandem represent a business opportunity by which market leaders are created or sustained.

The ground is not littered with companies which have realised that quality goals must extend to marketing. Most use quality thinking and techniques to affect their product or service base, leaving their sales and marketing stuck in the same old rut. It just will not do. However, oddly, the reverse is more likely to be true: total quality marketing methods can work for organisations not operating a total quality management regime. This is because in either case total quality marketing methods replace outdated, misguided methods which do not sufficiently respect the Customer. This is another reason why total quality marketing is what has to come next in selling, advertising and marketing.

Whatever the rights, wrongs, weaknesses or risks of the IBM, Rank Xerox and Royal Insurance experiences, all three companies carry the honours of pioneers – particularly because of their recognition that their marketing, as well as their products or services, should benefit the Customer. But surely the most important point in all this is that they have demonstrated that quality thinking does not stop at the doors of the sales and marketing departments.

Part Five: On the Road to Quality

24

The Should You, Shouldn't You Bit

The road to total quality marketing is long, hard and paved with hazards and conundrums. However, as you have seen by now, it's a good road, a worthwhile road and, most of all, an exquisitely profitable road in the long term. All you have to do is get it right.

Well, maybe it's a tightrope, not a road; we're as far as we can go down the quantity end and we've got to get back along the quality end.

Whichever way you picture it, the questions that must be in our minds now are: Should we do it? Indeed, why should we do it? How much of it should we do? What's in it for us if we do or don't? Let's consider the answers.

Should we do it?

There seems little doubt that the business world, indeed the whole world, accelerated by the usual charming forces of human nature – greed, envy, lust, fear, etc! – is set to continue along its precarious path. Only faster. When you look at the power balance and spread of material resources; the numbers and geography of haves and have-nots, there is little short-term good news, globally speaking. Anyway, life is full of spice, interest and intrigue. That's why you find that freedom comes to the Eastern Bloc, on the one hand, while the world is plunged into crisis in the Gulf, on the other. History offers testimony to such trials and tribulations. OK, but life goes on. We marketers must get on with the job. So we must; but, increasingly, our job will have to do with the provision of safety and security. That's why it's important that we understand that we can only deliver quality to our Customers if it keeps us healthy and provides for our own welfare and wellbeing. Quality is not a philanthropic issue, or even, at this stage, a moral issue. It's a survival and success issue.

The concept of three-way marketing lashed to the objective of relationship-building is the practical formula which provides the vehicle for survival, stability and success. Thus, we must look next at what is needed to build and nurture our all-important relationships.

I maintain that there is little difference between the needs of a corporate relationship and those of personal ones. They're both fun, rewarding, satisfying, fulfilling and damned hard work to get right. Perhaps that's why, corporately, so many people are busy screwing each other – in the quality world, we make corporate love!

So what qualities must we supply to our Customers, along with our products and services, to build the relationships we need? Trust. Respect. Integrity. Affection. These are the ingredients which build personal relationships. Why should corporate relationships be any different? In my view, the more number-crunching, data-processing and electronic transfers that go on – the more these human values will move into focus. The more robots, computers, machines and systems we devise, the more those things which actually win the business will revolve around the people. The electronics and the technology, after all, breed only short-term distinctions or competitive edges. In the long term they are levellers. Ultimately, success and prosperity are people issues. Importantly, it must be understood, that quality is entirely a people issue. Quantity builds sales. Quality builds friends for your business.

Reading the signs

You can see this already happening. Businesses, drowning under the expectations placed upon them by their Customers and pushed relentlessly forward by their competitors, are looking for friends. People to help. Partners. People to share and commit themselves to each other. Customers appreciate those who get closer and more intimate as the service standards reach levels of excellence and customisation never before achieved.

Intimacy, getting close, even making corporate love were not words or notions used in business a great deal in the decades of quantity. In those decades I was called an expert. Now I am told I'm a guru. So is all this guruspeak, idealistic lunacy, or is it what's going to happen?

On that issue, I will leave you to make up your mind. After all, by now you know mine! All my marketing experience and the years of research that have gone into this project convince me that total quality marketing is not a movement you can stop. It is a movement which will, over the coming years, preoccupy all honest, professional and ethical businesses. You can make up your mind about the rest, just as will their Customers.

A compelling business issue

When I put myself in the place of a prospect considering two competitors, I ask questions. Of course! But not just about the product, services, back-up, or country of origin ... I ask increasingly probing questions. After all, I am looking to be able to trust and respect these people. Finally, I ask myself this fascinating question:

> Do I want to do business with ...
> A COMPANY THAT PAYS ITS PEOPLE TO EXPLOIT ME?
> Or do I want to do business with ...
> A COMPANY THAT PAYS ITS PEOPLE TO SATISFY ME?

This is one of those questions to which you know the answer before you ask. It comes as a simultaneous bolt of lightning. It is a question Customers will ask in droves. They already are. That's why financial services people in the UK and other countries have to show their commission levels with certain contracts. That's why, as an old-fashioned, commission-driven, quantity salesperson, I would pray I didn't come up against anyone from Rank Xerox.

Ultimately you may have no real choice about whether you accept total quality marketing. The world will force it upon you. The questions are when and to what extent. For, as well as considering what accepting the quality ethic in relation to your marketing says about you, you must also consider what ignoring it says about you.

Is quality good for you?

Perhaps this is the more interesting issue. Since we can see that total quality marketing is what must come next for selling, advertising and marketing, the next question is, is it good for us – the marketers?

I believe the answer is yes; emphatically, yes. This is just another pressure to push us all down an inevitable channel. At the end both sides win. The Customer wins. But they were supposed to anyway. And the marketers win – at least the ones who get there first do.

I talked earlier of the quality lock. It locks Customers to you. It locks competitors out. For, that is the nature of marketing through relationships, not transactions; that is the result of satisfaction marketing, not exploitation selling.

It gets worse before it gets better

We looked at three qualities that are necessary to make the switch to total quality marketing: time, courage and money. You need the money to invest in the reintroduction of quality standards, ethics and thinking; you need time to plan and implement all the changes that need to be made; and you need courage to stick it out.

The fact is that as you make the transition, things get worse before they get better. This is why the ideal time to make the switch is from a position of strength when things are going well, rather than as a corrective or panic measure in the hope of a boost to business. It doesn't, it can't happen like that. Indeed, this is why companies that have adopted the quality ethic in relation to their production or service base, and have begun to see the benefits in productivity and performance, will find total quality marketing such a natural follow-on to total quality management. What more natural way to take your quality product to market than through quality marketing methods! In fact, it's a great shame there is such a wide gap between current marketing methods and quality market-ing methods, since it pays no compliment at all to the valuable and valued efforts which companies all over the world are making to strive, first for quality, and then onwards to perfection. Such a noble ultimate goal. Why should marketing get left behind?

However, this apparently simple change of process, concen-trating on what we do *for* Customers rather than what we do *to* them, needs careful thought. For business will go down at first. Performance will drop. Then it levels off and starts to climb. For the managers planning change, quantifying this curve will be all-important.

Step 1: know where you are;
Step 2: know where you want to be;
Step 3: understand the gap.

Success will depend on critical analysis and control of these factors: how far will success drop, how long is the plateau, how high will it climb, and at what rate or angle of ascent?

While the numbers and monetary values should be calculated and included in the case put to any board in support of total quality marketing, it is important that the benefits be fully considered; that is, not just the profits or ROCE figures or whatever your yardstick, but the fact, in these hard times ahead, that you will be keeping yours while all about are losing theirs!

What will be the engines of the total quality marketing movement?

I shall certainly be one! And so, no doubt, will Pip Mosscrop and his team at Collinson Grant. But, more seriously, what will be the key mechanisms that enable the changeover. I see them as the following:

- Harnessing technology, the development of hybrids and the welcoming of IT people to marketing.

- The acceptance of the need for and provision of total communications management.

- The integration of marketing into a fused, strategic process, the focus on marketing productivity, and the understanding of how and why marketing is different from selling.

- The realisation of their absolute power by Customers. And their experiments with that power.

- The overwhelming evidence that in the business climate of at least the immediate decade, quantity goals will do more harm than good.

The need to make fast, urgent decisions

We started out together thinking about the information that the forthcoming years are years of chaotic change, and change with relentless rapidity. Certainty is a diminishing value. It is said, there is no such thing as safe.

I disagree. Safe is achievable, but it has to be worked at. Total quality marketing is the work.

Those companies that survive, let alone succeed, will have taken, as many of them can be seen to be doing right now, far-reaching steps to be sure they can weather the storms. In this context you can predict the factors which will build resilience and durability. They are:

1. *Flexibility*: can you reshape, regroup, replan, respond and react with intelligence and alacrity?

2. *Team spirit*: do you encourage and reward the commitment and effectiveness of both the corporate and Client-serving team?

3. *Understanding*: hearing is not enough. Seeing, listening, and caring are vital too. Is your company ready to go for share of market achieved by share of mind?

4. *Obsession*: This goes beyond dedication, commitment, and service, because the obsession is with perfection.

Also it is possible to single out the key elements for the survival of your business, those things which will unlock the total quality marketing door for you.

1. *Cultural*: can you transform your market and your ethics to the know-how- and information-based era?

2. *Method*: how soon can you restructure, re-educate and realign towards multidiscipline marketing?

3. *Style*: how fast can you successfully adopt a 'relationship orientation' complete with the prerequisite database capability?

Don't doubt the urgency or the critical nature of these. And do not question their validity. Those who already know, who already understand, who already accept are way ahead of you.

I've decided – it's not for me!

Abandon hope all ye who feel this way. I beg you to take it as read that marketing must join the rest of the business world and embrace quality, not only as our approach to work, but also more importantly, as how we think about Customers.

The fact is that most organisations spend too much money on advertising and marketing. They shower money on prospecting which everyone who is honest knows is wasteful. Although, generally, and for many, the return from money spent on marketing to Customers is somewhere between 5 to 15 times greater, yet it is the conquest business and the prospecting which dominates our spending and our strategy, while returning the lowest possible value you can get from the marketing unit of currency.

During the last 30 years, as a result of misguided and greedy thinking, marketing has become a high-speed, high-cost business. It is technologically backward and in many ways a decidedly inferior corporate investment. It will get worse unless you and I do something about it.

For many people involved in marketing, either in small businesses, or at the other end of the scale in large FMCG businesses, it is so easy, too easy, to lean back and say 'Yes. OK. But it's not really for us.' To the smaller business I say this: we talked at the very beginning about the craftsman, a one-man business that cannot see any difference between its craft and the Customer's need. Ask yourself why so many big businesses are trying so hard to break themselves down to a network of organisations just like yours! It's because you are the perfect organisation to get close to Customers, to work with them, to understand their needs and respond quickly. One of the greatest accelerators of the total quality marketing concept is the envy so many people have of the effectiveness of the small business in these respects.

As for the FMCG fraternity, I urge you to stay in control of your margin, listen to the real Customer, and make your brand a, no, *the* quality brand.

But, lastly, may I say something to you, whatever the size of your business, whoever your Customer is, however you feel about quality issues. I'd like to say, thank you for taking the time to make friends with these ideas. I hope they'll serve you as well as the statement at the beginning of this book has served me. It has been my personal approach to business since I was grown up enough to have one.

Thank you for joining me on this wonderful and challenging, and, I hope, for you, provocative and stimulating journey into the minds of tomorrow's Customers. On which note, perhaps, I can leave you with one final thought. It's overleaf ...

The Customer is a holy cow.
You don't milk a holy cow.
You worship it.

Bibliography

Albrecht, Karl (1988) *At America's Service*, Dow Jones Irwin, New York.

Barham, Kevin and Rassan, Clive (1989) *Shaping the Corporate Future*, Unwin Hyman Ltd, London.

Dunn Humby Associates 'Use and attitudes to computers in marketing' (research document), Dunn Humby Associates, London.

Forrest, Philip (1987) *Sold on Service*, Carlson Marketing Group International, Northampton.

Fraser-Robinson, John (1989) *The Secrets of Effective Direct Mail*, McGraw-Hill Book Company Ltd, Maidenhead.

Jaques, Elliot (1989) *The Requisite Organisation. The CEO's Guide to Creative Structure and Leadership*, Cason Hall, Gower Press, Aldershot.

Harrison and Theaker (1989) *Dealing with Conflict*, Guild House Press, Whalley.

Liederman, Robert (1990) *The Telephone Book: How to find, get, keep and develop customers*, McGraw-Hill Book Company Ltd, Maidenhead.

Levitt, Theodore (1986) *The Marketing Imagination*, The Free Press, a division of Macmillan Inc, New York.

Lynch, Richard (1990) *European Business Strategies*, Kogan Page Ltd, London.

McCorkell, Graeme (1990) *Advertising That Pulls Response*, McGraw-Hill Book Company Ltd, Maidenhead.

Naisbitt, John and Aburdene, Patricia (1990) *Megatrends 2000*, Sidgwick & Jackson Ltd, London.

Oakland, John S (1989) *Total Quality Management*, Heinemann Professional Publishing Ltd, Oxford.

Ohmae, Kenichi (1990) *The Borderless World: Power and Strategy in the Interlinked Economy*, Collins, London.

Peters, Thomas J and Austin, Nancy (1986) *A Passion for Excellence*, Fontana, London.

Peters, Thomas J and Waterman, Robert H (1982) *In Search of Excellence*, Harper & Row Inc, New York.

Peters, Thomas J (1988) *Thriving on Chaos*, Macmillan Ltd, London.

Pettigrew, Andrew M (1988) *The Management of Strategic Change*, Basil Blackwell, Oxford.

Sveiby, Karl Erik and Lloyd, Tom (1987) *Managing Knowhow*, Bloomsbury Publishing Ltd, London.

Index